Living Beyond the POSSIBLE

Trusting God with your finances and your future

By
Wayne Myers
with
Mary Dunham Faulkner

Living Beyond the Possible
copyright © 2003 by Wayne Myers and Mary Dunham Faulkner

Published by Wayne Myers, The Great Commission Evangelistic Association
441 Fawn Ridge Apt 208
Dallas, TX 75224

All Scripture quotations, unless otherwise indicated, are the author's paraphrase of commonly known verses in The Holy Bible.

Scripture quotations marked AMPLIFIED are taken from The Amplified ® Bible, Copyright © 1954, 1958, 1962, 1965, 1987 by the Lockman Foundation. Published by Zondervan Publishing House. Used by permission. (www.Lockman.org)

Scripture quotations marked KJV are taken from the King James Version of the Bible.

Scripture quotations marked NIV are taken from the Holy Bible, New International Version ®. Copyright © 1973, 1978, 1984 by International Bible Society. Used by permission of Zondervan Publishing House. All rights reserved. The "NIV" and "New International Version" trademarks are registered in the United States Patent and Trademark Office by International Bible Society.

Scripture quotations marked NKJV are taken from the New King James Version. Copyright © 1879, 1980, 1982 by Thomas Nelson, Inc. Used by permission. All rights reserved.

Scripture quotation marked PHILLIPS is from J.B. Phillips, The New Testament in Modern English. Copyright © 1960 by J. B. Phillips. Printed in Great Britain by Cox & Wyman Ltd., Reading for the publishers Geoffrey Bles Ltd., 52 Doughty Street, London, WC1. Used by permission. All rights reserved.

ISBN: 0-9728048-0-3
Second Printing January 2004
Third Printing April 2008
Printed in Colombia

From the depth of my heart I dedicate this book to my wife, Martha, and our three children, David, Rebecca, and Paula, who are such a part of every victory won in His name.

FOREWORD

Who is this tall, thin, former U.S. sailor from World War II, now turned missionary? To gather information on him, I turned to my dependable diary, and there the first mention of Wayne Myers said that he arrived for our Christ For The Nations' (CFNI) Annual Seminar on August 10, 1969. On the twelfth, it reports that Myers took his first offering at CFNI for Native Churches, with "over sixty sponsors." On the sixteenth, Myers helped me raise $29,000 for Christian Center, the former nightclub we had agreed to purchase for $120,000 and which would become the base for Christ For The Nations Institute. The seminar was actually being held there and turned out to be greatly anointed of God.

Wayne Myers traveled with my husband, Gordon, and me in the U.S., as we presented the need of securing sponsors for Native Churches worldwide. Myers spoke with great compassion as he described the need, especially in Mexico, where he had actually started his ministry. When Gordon died suddenly in 1973 of a heart attack, Wayne and his wife, Martha, immediately stood with me, and from then on helped share the load of this ministry.

As soon as our Bible school opened in 1970, Wayne, as a guest speaker, was invited to come for a week each semester, challenging the students for a walk of faith. He has become a "regular."

As CFNI continued to grow, in 1976 our board voted to proceed building the Student Learning Center on our campus. Only one problem: we had no funds. On August 10, as I presented the need to the audience, Wayne Myers took the microphone and shocked us all as he declared: "Martha and I will pledge $100,000!" Others present accepted the challenge and $400,000 was raised in cash and pledges, inspired chiefly by Myers. The pledgees fulfilled their commitment ahead of schedule and the much-needed Student Center was built and paid for.

Some 29,000 students from over 100 countries have attended Christ For The Nations Institute, and nearly 100 percent have heard and been motivated to obey the Bible as Myers challenges them to give.

Myers' pithy, powerful, pointed, energetic messages captivate the attention of the students immeasurably. He himself is the supreme example. Without owning a home of his own, and driving a car that is usually given to him, it seems that "money grows in his pockets." As he walks on campus among the students, God often lays it on his heart to give to someone, and he obediently pulls out a ten or twenty dollar bill for that student. I've witnessed that many times.

When students are asked who their favorite speaker of the year is? You guessed it: Wayne Myers. This man of God is "one of a kind."

He has helped build over 4,000 native churches in Mexico alone, plus he has been vital in helping us build in many other nations—now over 11,000 native churches. God be praised!

Wayne and Martha Myers will have a great reward in heaven. I'd love to have a mansion next door to theirs!

A treasury of true experiences in the life of this humble, twentieth century apostle, Wayne Myers, whose practical yet powerful faith has influenced three generations to believe naturally for the supernatural, is the story of Living Beyond the Possible. It will revolutionize your life.

Freda Lindsay
Co-founder, Christ for the Nations Institute

TABLE OF CONTENTS

Introduction
Living to Give   xi

Chapter 1
True Prosperity   17

Chapter 2
Thieves and Robbers   23

Chapter 3
Daily Deposits in Eternal Accounts   31

Chapter 4
Start With What You Have   41

Chapter 5
A Spoon and a Shovel   49

Chapter 6
Seeing the Invisible   57

Chapter 7
Obedient Giving   65

Chapter 8
Living and Giving Through Faith   73

Chapter 9
Faith Promises   79

Chapter 10
Giving Beyond the Possible   89

Chapter 11
Giving With a Willing Heart   101

Chapter 12
Giving God Something Precious   109

Chapter 13
Giving With the Right Motive   117

Chapter 14
Giving Out of Our Need   123

Chapter 15
Giving God More Than Money   131

Chapter 16
Sacrificial Giving   141

Chapter 17
Unlimited Potential   149

Chapter 18
Born to Win   155

INTRODUCTION

Living to Give

Kuala Lumpur is a hot, beautiful city in Malaysia with some of the world's tallest buildings and oldest Muslim mosques. But when my wife, Martha, and I visited there several years ago, we were hardly interested in the buildings. Our mission was the same one we've been on for over fifty-six years in hundreds of cities around the globe. We were in Malaysia to love people and to teach them the secret of the ultimate lifestyle of living to give.

If our target was to touch people, we had obviously come to the right place. Over one million of Kuala Lumpur's population are descendants from multiple ancient cultures and backgrounds and worship almost as many different religious gods. Malay, Indian, Chinese, Arab, and Portuguese are steeped in Hinduism, Buddhism, Animism, and Taoism.

Thank God for the Christians there who are reaching out to their nation. I spoke to just under one thousand Chinese, Malaysian, and Indian believers in the tearoom of the historic Majestic Hotel in the heart of Kuala Lumpur. Even though the congregation was made up of professionals and students from the University of Malaysia, the price of real estate was so high the members couldn't afford to buy their own building.

Or so they thought. I knew better. I was there to build their faith to be able to see the invisible, which in this case was their building. I challenged them to give towards their own church by faith, making a promise to believe God to supply what they did not have. By the time I left, we had raised $650,000 (American currency) in faith promises.

It's a radical way to live, a radical way to give. But I've seen the kingdom of God advance all over the world through people who step out of the ordinary in order to experience the supernatural. As for that church in Malaysia, the supernatural meant stepping into a dream they thought was impossible. All of those promised offerings came in. Now they own their own building with a seating capacity of 1,800 people.

When I visited their church a few years later, they were having five services every Sunday in their new location—two in the Malay language, one in English, one in Chinese, and one in the Korean language. I met one of their members a few years later when I was in Canada, speaking in a church in Vancouver.

"Do you remember the time you spoke in Malaysia?" The question was from a sharp-looking Chinese man who introduced himself as an oral surgeon who lived in the area.

"How could I forget!" I responded, relieved that he didn't ask me if I remembered him.

"I was a student at the University of Malaysia when you challenged us to give. It changed my life."

I meet them in my travels all over the world—people who have discovered the secret of living to give instead of living to get.

I've seen this message change thousands of lives from the Amazon of Peru to the slums of Nairobi, Kenya. The principles that I'm going to share with you are still changing lives all over the world. If you are financially challenged, this book is for you. And if you have more money than you know what to do with, well, it is especially for you. The truths that are laid out in the Bible for us on this subject are revolutionary. I know. I live by them.

In fact, Martha and I are wealthy. I know what you're thinking, and no, we don't drive a Lexus or own several homes around the world. I've never considered the accumulation of material goods to be a true barometer of prosperity. I don't have time to grab for things I can only keep for seventy-five or one hundred years. Have you ever seen a hearse pulling a U-Haul? I haven't.

In fact, all that my wife and I own of this world's goods are a few perishable items that won't be of any use to us in eternity—two cars and some furniture. And to tell you the truth, that's all we need. Our earthly treasures have no price tag: three children and nine grandchildren who make us proud, friends who stand with us day in and day out in all kinds of circumstances, our health, and the honorable position of being a servant to the ministers and churches around the globe who are changing the world. You don't have enough money to buy any of these treasures from me.

For me, prosperity is going to sleep at night without sleeping pills, and having all of my investments in a heavenly account where the interest rates are three, six, and ten thousand percent. Prosperity is bringing souls into the kingdom, and seeing my tiny seed grow into productive lives all around the globe. God's prosperity is having your own needs met with enough left over to bless others in need.

The pattern began with Jesus (who gave everything that He had) and the early church (who sold their possessions and gave the money to expand the kingdom). The early Christians knew their possessions were not their own. Everything we have is from God, the Giver.

Many years ago Martha and I determined we would give a monetary gift on an average of every day of the 365 days of a year. Some days it's not very much. Other days it may be a large check. Whatever we have, we give accordingly.

Some people say, "Wayne, you can't live like that. You'll go broke." And I tell them, "Listen, I was broke when I started giving. I haven't been broke since." Not many people understand the joy that comes from living a life of giving. Once you start this walk, you're hooked for life. Call me self-serving if you want to, but the fact is, giving makes me happy.

Most of us look for joy in all the wrong places, accumulating more things that never make us happy but only tie us down. On the other hand, giving changes our focus from ourselves to the needs of others. It's a biblical principle that has always been the key to contentment and deep joy. Listen to this verse from the Old Testament that shows us the formula for joy:

"The people rejoiced...for they had given freely and wholeheartedly to the LORD" (1 Chronicles 29:9 NIV).

I call it the source of vitamin J and you can't find it in a health food store. Not many of us associate joy with giving, though we often quote Jesus who said that it is more blessed to give than to receive.

"The liberal soul shall be made fat, and he that waters shall also be watered himself" (Proverbs 11:25) is more than a theory. It is a proven principle of God's ability to take care of those who are willing to give themselves away for His cause.

Money is an instrument that can buy
you everything but happiness and pay
your fare to everywhere but heaven.

"Everything in your hand is a seed.
Everything in God's hand
is a harvest."

Before Martha and I married, I lived in Mexico as a single man without money, a decent car, nor a house of my own. During one lean season, I lived in the back of a poor little Mexican church in Veracruz with a friend who was just getting started in the ministry. Both of us were full of zeal and a simple faith that trusted God for our next meal. A Christian lady who lived across the street in a small, dilapidated house seemed wealthy by comparison. She had a tile floor, chickens that supplied her eggs, and a pig that would eventually go to market.

She invited us to stay in her little home for two months while she went out of town, making us an offer we couldn't refuse. "If you'll feed the chickens and the pig and pay the light bill, you can live in my house," she told us.

My friend and I had been roughing it for so long that the little house seemed like a Holiday Inn. The house had a small kerosene stove and one bedroom with a double bed. We had chickens to supply us with eggs, a stove to cook our food, and a tile floor with no splinters. This was uptown!

After a few days we realized that there was a slight downside to this whole scene. For starters, even though our friend had a number of hens, only one chicken laid any eggs. That wasn't really as big of a problem as much as *where* she laid her eggs.

Every day with great ceremony, that chicken walked through the kitchen door. Clucking loudly, she proceeded through the living room, made a right turn into the bedroom, jumped on the bed, and laid an egg. We were sleeping in her nest.

After a few days of observing this strange ceremonial offering, I'd had enough. I met her at the door with a broom and announced, "Mrs. Hen, there's a new administration. You'll have to find somewhere else to lay your eggs."

She did, but in the process, she hid her nest—which meant no more eggs for my breakfast. On top of that, the pig had an insatiable appetite. Not only were we not getting eggs anymore, but also our operating expenses had increased. Now we were feeding hens that didn't lay eggs, financially supporting a fat pig, and paying the light bill. Our meager budget did not stretch far enough for the two of us to eat. It was a tight time.

One day the hen showed up at our door. I quickly took advantage of the situation and said, "Mrs. Hen, I owe you an apology. You were here before I was. The house is yours. Come on in!" She did, and we began to have our eggs again.

Finally, we were down to our last supply of beans. They must have been pre-war, because you could boil them all day and they would still roll like marbles. Manuel and I took turns cooking, although I'm not sure why—no matter who cooked them, they were hard and unseasoned.

One day it was my turn to cook the beans, so I put them on the stove to boil while we had our daily prayer meeting. Both Manuel and I prayed so fervently that we forgot the boiling pot on the stove. A scorched odor filled the small house and I knew that I had burned the last of our bean supply.

"It appears the Lord wants us to fast today," I told Manuel. I tried to cheer us both by saying how much easier it would be to fast without food in the house to tempt us. It did little good to alter the facts: we were out of food.

A few hours later there was a knock on the door. One of the neighborhood women who had never spoken to us, was standing there with tamales and corn on the cob. For Manuel and me, it was a banquet from heaven.

There's one advantage to having scarce funds—it can lubricate your knees toward prayer. We were both learning lessons about God and how to survive on His faithfulness alone. Neither of us would trade those experiences. Manuel, who couldn't speak English when I met him, went on to Bible school in Los Angeles and eventually received his Masters degree in Germany. He learned seven languages and returned to his native tribe, the Totonac Indians, and built a school and a Bible school.

Recently, Martha and I preached to those same Indians and saw the tremendous impact Manuel's life had on them. He was a soul winner who had traveled the world and won thousands of converts to Christ. When he died a few years ago, he left his mark not only in Mexico, but also around the world.

> *A person who constantly accumulates and hoards because of a fear of going without, lives in bondage to the fear of poverty.*

If Manuel or I had been looking for the kind of prosperity that some ministries define as proof of God's blessing—new cars, comfortable homes, and fat bank accounts—we would have missed the great adventure of a life call for both of us.

I have always said that if money is our reason for living, and if we gauge our worth by what we have and not by what we give, we have no reason to live. Unless our goal is to seek God's kingdom first, we have no goals that are worth our time nor effort.

When do you know if you have enough money? I know wealthy people with a poverty complex. A poverty complex is not defined by a shortage of funds, but rather a heart attitude. A person who constantly accumulates and hoards because of a fear of going without, lives in bondage to the fear of poverty. If we constantly worry about losing what we don't need, in all probability we will. If you are saving for a rainy day, hold onto it, because you're going to get wet. If you doubt God's faithfulness to provide, Satan will rob you of peace and trust in God. Being so attached to our possessions or bank account that we can't release either could never be mistaken for the over-flowing, abundant lifestyle that God designed for us to live.

On the other hand, there are people who live on meager incomes. Yet they are rich in a faith that their needs will be supplied. They have an active, dependent trust in God to supply the money for the bills that accumulate each month and for food to put on the table. As an added bonus to an often exercised faith, they don't have a surplus to worry about. Their lives are simple and fruitful.

Who would you say is prospering?

Of all of our blessings, Martha and I are richest in our family and friends. I can testify of knowing people who embrace a lifestyle of trusting God for what they need and give away the surplus. They are doing exploits for God and making an impact on nations around the world. Not only are they watching their dreams unfold, they are also seeing God supply an abundance for others through them.

When Jesus said it was more blessed to give than to receive, He was speaking from His knowledge of how He created us—to be givers, like Him. God will always prosper you with this purpose: He wants you to bless someone else.

John Maxwell tells the story of a popular French author who went to India to do research for a new book which became a best seller. He had become wealthy through his writing, and arrived in India with a new Rolls Royce. When he saw the poverty and misery, he was charged by a passion to do something about it. Now he divides his time between writing, fund-raising, and donating money to help the plight of the poor. On the back of his business card he has printed, "All that is not given is lost."

Wealth alone has never made anyone happy. Millionaire John D. Rockefeller is quoted as saying, "I have made millions, but they have brought me no happiness."

True prosperity is to know God intimately as our provider for everything we need. It's falling asleep at night without a sleeping pill, and waking up to unlimited possibility. Prosperity is a lifestyle that doesn't hang on to the temporal, but constantly gives away what is impossible to keep for the long haul. It's watching our gifts and talents and influence multiply and grow, like my friend Manuel who left this world with a host of believers who became Christians because of his life.

THIEVES AND ROBBERS

2

Give according to your income
lest God reduces your income
according to your giving.

It was after midnight in Puebla, Mexico and I had just finished speaking at a large Christian conference. I was exhausted from the long hours of teaching, but needed to be back home by morning. I had no alternative but to get started on the two-hour drive back to Mexico City.

Nine of my Mexican brothers and I set out for home in my 1965 Chevrolet station wagon. I knew we would be traveling on narrow, winding roads through mountain passes—a desolate area where robbers waited for unsuspecting drivers to pass through their war zone. Unscrupulous and dangerous, these men would often drag a large tree across the road, which forced drivers to stop. When all of the occupants of the car were completely at their mercy, they would rob them of their handbags and luggage, helping themselves to watches, money, and anything else that looked valuable.

"Lord, have mercy on us tonight," I prayed with my friends. "Keep us from the robbers while we make this journey." I was glad I had the company of my Mexican brothers to keep me awake and to help pray.

Chanito sat in the front seat with me. He was the son of a murderer and no stranger to the ways of highway bandits. He never went to school, never had parental love, but was a dynamic preacher who loved God. He was one of the young men I discipled in Mexico and was also one of Martha's and my dear friends. In fact, he had saved my life on three different occasions; I literally owed my life to him.

I had spoken on the subject of giving in the convention and our conversation that night just naturally turned to finances and giving. Chanito confided that he never seemed to have enough money. I immediately knew the root of his problem.

"You don't tithe, do you, Chanito?" I asked him.

"All I know is that God has power to provide," he responded.

"Yes, I know God has power," I shot back. "But I asked you, do you tithe?"

"I believe in the power of God," Chanito hedged again.

"Chanito, you didn't answer my question." I was irritated with his evasiveness.

"Brother Wein, I don't have enough money to tithe," his confession came out in a whiny complaint.

I jerked the car over to the side of the road and came to a complete stop.

"Get out of God's car," I commanded.

We were under a blanket of black night, miles from the nearest town, and completely vulnerable to whatever or whoever might be lurking in the darkness.

"Why?" Chanito's voice was incredulous.

"Because I'm harboring a thief and you are endangering my life."

He was in a dazed state of shock, standing outside the car and surrounded by thick darkness. I could tell he still couldn't believe this was happening. "You're not going to leave me with the thieves, Brother Wein," he implored.

Chanito had heard me teach on giving, and knew that according to the Bible, he should tithe. Obviously, he had no intention of heeding my message given at the convention. What better place than to teach it again?

"Let the thieves beware of you!" I told him. " I'm more afraid of you than I am of them. They only rob men. You have the audacity to rob God."

"Brother Wein, I promise I will start tithing." Chanito was

negotiating his ride back to Mexico City.

"All right, get in," I conceded. Of course, I would not have left him for a minute on that road. But he got the point. Chanito climbed back in the car, subdued and quiet. I knew my object lesson had hit home.

Chanito learned to tithe, and in the end, money was only a small part of what he gave God. He is in heaven now, but before he died, he established congregations in the most difficult parts of Mexico where life is worth very little.

A lot of people are like Chanito—they think they can't afford to tithe. I tell them they can't afford *not* to tithe. I can't imagine a more risky way to live than taking what belongs to God. Please don't think that God is nonchalant about whether you give Him ten percent of your income or not. Listen to His words on the matter:

"Will a man rob God? Yet you have robbed Me!

But you say, 'In what way have we robbed You?'

"In tithes and offerings. You are cursed with a curse, for you have robbed Me, even this whole nation. Bring all the tithes into the storehouse, that there may be food in My house, and try Me now in this, says the Lord of hosts, if I will not open for you the windows of heaven and pour out for you such blessing that there will not be room enough to receive it" (Malachi 3: 8-10 NIV).

Every time that offering plate passes in front of you and God's tithe is in your pocket, it is a form of theft. I am amazed at Christians who love God, but who ignore this basic discipline of faith.

I spoke on tithing to a congregation of 2,500 people in Mexico City. I explained the verse in Malachi, which says that withholding tithes is a form of robbing God. And then I did something I've never done before. I gave an altar call for thieves who had robbed

God. Nearly 500 people stood up, convicted by the Holy Spirit for not tithing. After I led them in a prayer of repentance, I gave them an opportunity to give their tithes to that church right then. The results were eight million pesos, or about $6,500 in U.S. currency.

None of that money was for me, nor my missionary projects. The money went back into the church where they were attending. I don't teach this message because I want people to give to me. I teach on giving tithes because it's in the Bible, and because I want Christians to know the blessing that comes from obedience to God's Word.

One of the times that I preached this message, a farmer came forward to tell me about the time his crop of corn was more sparse than usual. In fact, he only made about 5,000 pesos from the whole crop, the equivalent of 400 American dollars. He knew he should give God 10 percent of that money, but it seemed too much for such a small profit.

"Tithing is foolish," a persuasive voice in his mind spoke. "Five hundred pesos is a lot of money, and besides, your pastor has new shoes and you don't."

The Christian farmer wrapped the five 1,000-peso bills in a handkerchief and walked out of the bank. A few minutes later, as he felt a sneeze coming on he jerked out his handkerchief. By the time he remembered the money he had tucked in it, it was too late. A strong gust of wind picked up the five bills and took his total income toward heaven. He failed to give the 500 pesos that would have been his tithes and ended up paying 4,500 pesos in back interest.

Not many of us have seen such a visual picture of what happens to our profit when we withhold God's portion. But the message is true for all of us: We lose when we try to hold on to that which does not belong to us. Could this be the reason that so many work and work and yet their credit cards are full-to-the-brim with debt? I tell people that the credit card is the greatest invention since the wheel; it turns thrift into instant greed. You buy things you don't need, with money you don't have, to impress people you don't like. Many of God's precious people need "plastic surgery."

> *We lose when we try to hold on to that which does not belong to us.*

God wants to increase your store in every area of your life. He wants you to be His hands extended, sharing and blessing others. Listen to what He is saying to you today:

"Try Me now in this, says the Lord of hosts, if I will not open for you the windows of heaven and pour out for you such blessing that there will not be room enough to receive it. And I will rebuke the devourer for your sakes, so that he will not destroy the fruit of your ground, nor shall the vine fail to bear fruit for you in the field," says the Lord of hosts; And all nations will call you blessed, for you will be a delightful land," says the Lord of hosts" (Malachi 3:10-12 NKJV).

That word from Malachi is for every culture, every nation, and every financial situation in the world. *Where did we get the idea that if we are poor God doesn't expect us to give tithes?*

I was preaching among the Indians, high up in the mountains of Mexico, a number of years ago. After giving Malachi's sermon, I said, "This afternoon, we are going to dedicate the tithes and first fruits to your pastor."

It was about 12:30 in the afternoon. One of the men from the congregation stepped up to me and said, "Could you wait until 3:00 P.M.? "

"Why?" I asked.

"See that little hut across that canyon? That's where I live. It's an hour's walk home and another hour back and it will only take me thirty minutes to find the goat I want to give God."

"I'll wait," I promised him.

He came with a little red goat on his arm, and that goat had no desire to be given away. It squirmed and bleated all the way up to the altar. We dedicated a large offering of forty-seven chickens and turkeys, nine goats and pigs, some money, and bags of beans. The pastor felt as though he had just come into a large inheritance.

Several years later, I traveled back to the same congregation. I asked about the brother who ran home to get his goat for God.

"How many goats did he have that day?" I asked the pastor.

"He had six goats and he gave one to God."

"And how many does he have now?" I kept probing.

The pastor laughed. "He's got goats jumping all over the mountainsides."

That's my God! He's no man's debtor. "Prove me in this," He urges us. "See what happens."

If you don't tithe, I encourage you to repent and obey. It's as easy as that. All of our giving must begin with this first step. We must give God what belongs to Him.

3

If you want to be rich—give.
If you want to be poor—hoard.
If you want to be needy—grasp.
If you want to have
abundance—scatter.

*"The real measure of our wealth
is how much we would be
worth if we lost it all."*

Carlos is a Mexican Christian who has been financially blessed beyond many of his Latin friends. When he decided to sell several of his homes, he asked his pastor for help. "Pastor, if you'll pray and ask God to help me sell these homes at good profit, I promise to bring the tithes back into the church," he told him.

The pastor prayed and the homes sold at a profit, just as Carlos had requested. But contrary to his promise, he decided to keep all the money for himself. He didn't even put the profit he made in the bank, but instead, stuffed it all under his mattress.

His bedroom was on the second floor of his house with a small balcony that overlooked the street below. One day his four-year-old-son discovered the mattress with the hidden treasure. Of course the boy had no concept of the value of what equaled thousands of dollars. He walked over to the balcony and happily blessed everyone who walked by. You can imagine the consternation of his father when he discovered what had happened to their nest egg. Not only was their money gone, but there was no way of recovering any of it. He had broken his promise to God and lost everything.

Most of us don't stuff our money under our mattresses, but according to the Bible, tucking it away in a bank isn't much safer:

"Lay not up for yourselves treasures upon earth, where moth and rust doth corrupt, and where thieves break through and steal: But lay up for yourselves treasures in heaven, where neither moth nor rust doth corrupt, and where thieves do not break through and steal: For where your treasure is, there will your heart be also" (Matthew 6:19-21 KJV).

INVEST IN THE ETERNAL

Unless you leave an inheritance in God's kingdom while you're on earth, you'll have a pauper's portion on your arrival on the other side. There's no way you can transfer funds from your bank down here to the bank of heaven after you say good-bye to this world. I tell people everywhere I go that, as people of God, we are highly privileged to live a life that constantly exchanges the earthly for the heavenly. We must daily live our lives with eternal values before us.

It is rare to find people who focus on the eternal instead of the temporal; yet it is the key to all of life. This is the lifestyle that enables you to live free in an encumbered world, happy in an unhappy world, blessed when everyone else is complaining. God's plan for His children has never been for us to fret over how we are going to make the next house payment. He wants us to have enough resources in our hand to bless and give to others in need.

The key to not living in fear of your financial future is to live one day at a time. In The Lord's Prayer, Jesus taught us to pray for our daily bread. I realize this is contrary to everything your financial planner has advised you, but Jesus said, *"Therefore I tell you, stop being perpetually uneasy (anxious and worried) about your life, what you shall eat or what you shall drink; or about your body, what you shall put on. Is not life greater [in quality] than food, and the body [far above and more excellent] than clothing?"* (Matthew 6: 25, AMPLIFIED).

I learned this truth at the beginning when God called me to live in Mexico for the cause of missions around the world. I was studying at Southern California Bible College in Pasadena, California, passionately involved with the work of God. I spent hours praying, preaching on the street, and handing out tracts to anyone who would take them from me. When I realized God was calling me to Mexico to live as a missionary…well, that was another thing altogether. What if I couldn't learn the language? How could I communicate God to people who not only had different customs but spoke another language? What about my health? I had survived many major stomach operations and the best Navy doctors said I would be on a specialized diet for the rest of my life. Then there was the question of finances. How was I going to live?

Still, I knew that surrendering to the will of God was my only choice. I had made a decision to give Him everything I had and everything I was. If He was calling me to live my life in Mexico, then I would go. There were no other options.

"God, I don't see how you can use my life," I prayed. "I don't qualify physically, scholastically, or theologically, but if you can use my life, I'm available."

One night after praying in the Spirit for three hours, I heard God's audible voice telling me to write down whatever He spoke. I quickly leafed through my Bible to find the five white index cards I had stuffed between the pages and began writing. The words came through clearly, addressing all three of the concerns I had prayed about. In regard to my health, the Lord reminded me that He was my Healer and would take care of me. True to His word, I have lived in divine health for fifty years. Regarding the language, He said that He would help me learn to speak to the people effectively. He has. Now, fifty-five years later, I actually communicate easier in Spanish than I do in English.

I will never forget His words He spoke to me about finances: *"Son, I own the cattle on a thousand hills and the gold therein. Keep your vertical lines open. Guard the motives of your heart. Do all for my glory. I'll take care of your horizontal needs and ministries."* His voice was so clear that I marked down the date—November 26, 1946.

God has kept His word to me for over fifty-six years. Martha and I have never lacked for what we have needed to raise a family and to do the work of God. Not only has He supplied for us, but He has allowed us the joy of watching others prosper. By God's grace we have helped build churches in many nations and have raised enough money to give more than 100 vehicles to deserving missionaries and national leaders who are involved in spreading the gospel of Jesus Christ. Nothing has given us greater joy than having a part in the global harvest.

The secret, I believe, is that I take seriously God's admonition to me those many years ago to guard the motives of my heart.

BE CAREFUL

In Luke 12:13, there is a story of two brothers arguing over inheritance money who finally take their quarrel to Jesus.

"Teacher, tell my brother to divide the inheritance with me," one of the men demands. But Jesus didn't take sides in the family fight. Instead, He went directly to the motives of the heart:

"Take heed and beware of covetousness, for one's life does not consist in the abundance of the things he possesses."

"Take heed...beware...be on your guard." He says the same thing to you and me today. If Jesus tells us to be on our guard against covetousness, He knows that we are susceptible to this spirit that identifies the mind-set of the world we live in. Fear and greed cause

us to hoard and save, to covet and stockpile. *Covetousness is a master that is never satisfied—no matter what we have there is always one more thing that we want.*

"*Whoever loves money never has money enough,*" the preacher says in Ecclesiastes 5:10 NIV. The same verse goes on to say, "*whoever loves wealth is never satisfied with his income.*" And then ends with God's thoughts on the whole matter…"*This too is meaningless.*"

> *Most of us know the price of everything and the value of nothing. The accumulation of "things that we gotta have" is Satan's trick to enslave us and cause us to miss the high mark of our calling.*

Most of us know the price of everything and the value of nothing. The accumulation of "things that we gotta have" is Satan's trick to enslave us and cause us to miss the high mark of our calling.

Many Christians have never had so much stuff and yet they enjoy it less. When we can't separate our need from our greed, we live enslaved to what we want and what we don't have. We lust for what is not ours. God, in His great wisdom, knew this attitude would rob us of heaven's best for our lives. "*I have seen a grievous evil under the sun: wealth hoarded to the harm of its owner*" (Ecclesiastes 5:13 NIV).

I've never been blessed by a hoarding, selfish Christian, have you? Neither has God.

GIVE UNTIL THE PAIN
GOES AWAY

The great antidote to greed is giving. One of my Mexican brothers once complained to me, "Every time I give an offering, I feel pain."

"There's a remedy, brother," I told him. " Keep giving until the pain disappears."

If you want to be poor, hoard. If you want to be needy, grasp. But if you want an abundance, scatter—after all, we only own what we give away. If you can't release it, it owns you and is opposite of the way of the Kingdom of God, which is to live with an open heart and an open hand. When we let go of what we have, we discover we don't need as much as we thought we did to be content. I'm not advocating poverty, or even an austere lifestyle, nor do I have a problem with God's children owning Cadillacs or beautiful homes.

True spiritual prosperity comes not by seeking those things, but rather by focusing on God who does not begrudge His children of pleasure. *"Seek ye first the kingdom,"* He admonishes us in Matthew 6:33 KJV, *"and all these things shall be added unto you."*

> *If you want to be poor, hoard. If you want to be needy, grasp. But if you want an abundance, scatter.*

A missionary on a very tight budget, who lived and worked with his family in the Marshall Islands, experienced this verse first-hand when he returned to the States. He and his wife had poured their money and energy into the work of God on the islands and came home without the funds to buy their own car. One of the Christians in his support group bought a Cadillac for the family and, of course, they were elated.

They were unprepared for the response from a group of conservative Christians who were shocked at "their lack of humility" in driving a luxury car. "How can you drive a Cadillac?" they questioned him.

"It drives like any other car, only better," was his reply.

"Yes, but you are a missionary." They still argued.

He said, "It's not mine."

"No? Then whose is it?"

"It's a company car."

As long as what you have belongs to "the company," enjoy it. Just keep a "For Sale" sign in the trunk, in case God needs it on short order.

Our attitude about our possessions determines if we are living with an eternal perspective or not. When we can hold everything loosely, recognizing that everything we have, including our breath, comes from Him, then God is able to entrust us with blessings that we could only dream about before.

HAND AND HEART COORDINATION

If you want an intimate relationship with God, be a giver, like God. I've never known a grasping Christian who had an ability to receive a revelation and appropriate truth while maintaining a self-absorbed lifestyle. It's amazing how our heart and hands are connected. When you open your hands, you open your heart to a deeper intimacy with God, who is known by His giving.

Jesus was a servant, ministering to the needs of people wherever He went. We are like Him when we move through life, watching for opportunities to bless others. You and I have much to give and it takes so little to make the difference in someone else's day. Tell someone you appreciate them, encourage someone, and pray for someone who is down. Practice putting a five or ten-dollar bill in your handshake or write out a check for the single mother or poor stranger passing through your church. If you don't have money, share your food or your time or your natural talents.

"I'll start to give just as soon as my ship comes in" is a common comment I often hear. I say, "Why wait?" Why not row your boat out and meet your blessing? If you don't have a boat, start swimming. Winning the lottery is a fantasy. Giving is a discipline. We don't have to have an abundance to begin, just a willing heart that says, "Everything I have comes from God. I will share it in obedience to Him."

The widow woman with two mites left to her name didn't wait until life became easier. She gave out of her poverty. Jesus said those last two mites were more than the rich man's offering of gold. You see, God counts the quality before He counts quantity. While we're looking at the amount of the check, He sees what's left on the check stub. *The quality of the gift reveals the quality of the giver.*

DAILY DILIGENCE

We are children of God, bound for eternity, and the best way to prepare for that transition is to make daily deposits in our heavenly bank account. Every time we give our tithe, every time we pray a prayer, every time we give a love-gift to someone, we make a deposit in our bank account in heaven.

We must live each day with eternal values if we are going to impact the Kingdom of God. Let me challenge you to seek the things that are above every day. Practice rejecting the world's system and all of its deception.

"...Aim at and seek the rich, eternal treasures that are above, where Christ is, seated at the right hand of God" (Col.3:1 AMPLIFIED).

Live with open hands. Live with an open heart. Bless somebody every day of your life. It will add a brand new dimension to your life. Acknowledge daily that life is more than things. Every day practice looking unto Jesus as the Author and Finisher of your faith and I guarantee it will cause this world to look like cheap costume jewelry in a second-hand pawnshop on Skid Row.

The smallest act of obedience
is better than the best of
intentions.

*"There are no victories
at bargain prices."*

When Martha and I visited the small southern African nation of Malawi several years ago, we flew to the border of Mozambique to hold a conference for the Christians of both nations. From our vantage point in the twin-engine Piper Aztec, we saw the results of a land ravaged by war and famine—280,000 refugees camped in the middle of a parched, red clay desert where water and food were scarce. Thousands of survivors had fled the war in Mozambique, and even though they were living in limbo, they were the fortunate ones who were fed by the United Nations. Multiple thousands of desperate Africans were starving while trying to scratch out a living in a barren land controlled by a hostile government.

Martha and I and our hosts, Rod and Ellie Hein, arrived at the church where the campaign was being held. We were greeted by the sounds of beating drums and 1,500 Africans singing and dancing. These Christians were proof of what I have taught all over the world: *Happiness is not based on what you have, but Who you know.*

Some dressed in rags, had walked for four days to get to the meetings, with little food to eat along the way. When we realized that it had been several years since they had tasted meat, we immediately arranged to buy two cows to feed them during the conference. I had no idea that they would slaughter the animals right there on the spot. There was nothing to do but preach while competing with the pitiful bleating of two reluctant sacrifices in the background.

Martha and I were honored to share in the Heins' ministry to these Africans who had survived drought and national chaos and still held on to their faith in God. I knew that the message I had shared in some of the wealthiest churches in the United States, Australia, South America, Europe, and Asia had the power to change the lives of these poverty-stricken, war-ravaged believers. But I needed courage—how could I tell such poor people to give?

I was looking into the eyes of some of the most desperate people in the world. But someone had to tell them that God's irrefutable laws would work for them just as it would for their fat, wealthy American brother. I shared the scriptures with them and challenged them to think of others.

"All of us can give something," I admonished them. "If all you have is a handful of peanuts, share a little with your neighbor, help someone lift their load, carry water for the older grandmother."

Suddenly there was a commotion in the crowd. I could hear the sounds but couldn't see what was causing everyone's attention to be drawn to the back of the crowd. I stopped speaking and asked Martha if she knew what was happening.

"It's Debbie, the Heins' nine-year-old daughter," she told me. "She's taken off her shoes and is trying them on the African children's feet, trying to find a fit so she can give them away."

Debbie's instant response to the message was no doubt registered in heaven as one of the quickest acts of obedience on earth. Her simple childlike innocence reasoned that she had something that her poor, barefoot friends needed, and so she gave what she had.

Her unselfish act was the perfect illustration for my sermon. That nine-year-old's spontaneous reaction that day is to me what giving is all about. She didn't have to weigh the pros and cons of giving up her shoes, nor was she concerned that she would be barefoot for the remaining days of our time at the border. Debbie didn't ask her parents if they were going to buy her another pair before she shared her own with an African girl who needed them. It was a gift from her heart.

When people tell me they would like to give but just aren't in a position to do so, I tell them about Debbie and the meeting in Malawi, Africa. All of us can give something. No one expected a nine-year-old girl to take care of the budget of feeding 1,500 hungry people. But she could share a pair of shoes.

You have to start from where you are with what you have. When you practice giving, you will naturally grow in the grace of giving. No one starts giving away $10,000 all at once, especially if $100 is the most you've given. But whatever you've given, begin to increase the amount. You will find that heavenly economics will settle your financial problems and give you so much to give that it will take more prayer to ask God where He wants you to plant your offering.

Just like everything else in your life of faith, God will guide you in the area of sharing your finances. When God speaks, obey Him. One step of obedience always opens up two doors—the door of supply and the door to serve. *God's best rewards are always the opportunities that He puts in your way.*

In Guatemala, I preached on giving to a group of 200 church members gathered in the ballroom of a Camino Real hotel. A little four-year-old boy named Alex sat beside his father, Pastor Jorge Lopez, and listened intently to the sermon. At the conclusion of my message, he raised his hand and said, "I'll give twenty quetzales (the equivalent of twenty dollars).

On their way home, his father asked, "Son, you raised your hand tonight and told Brother Myers that you were going to give twenty quetzales. I'm proud of you for wanting to give, but where are you going to get the money?"

"Daddy, I have money in my piggy bank," he told his dad.

When they arrived home, they found the piggy bank, broke it

open, and counted the money together—eleven dollars and fifty cents.

Alex started praying that God would give him the eight dollars and fifty cents to pay his commitment, and sure enough, he turned in his offering on time. Today Alex co-pastors a 12,000-member church with his dad in Guatemala City.

Obedience always opens doors and enlarges our destiny. But fear is the enemy of obedience. The great enemy of giving is a fearful attitude. Some people are afraid that if they give their portion away, they won't have enough for themselves. The world is so negative, so fearful, that if you're not careful, the negativity will rub off on you. Don't let fear rob you of the future and destiny that God has for you. Romans 12:2 says it well: *"Don't let the world around you squeeze you into its own mould."* (PHILLIPS).

Do you remember the widow at Zarephath who was so poor that she only had enough food for one last meal for herself and her son? She was gathering sticks at the town gate to build a fire when the prophet, Elijah, asked her for a drink of water. As she turned to fetch the water, he casually added, "Oh, and bring me, please, a piece of bread."

What seemed like a casual, logical request for anyone else was a devastating reminder to her that she was going to die. She had run out of resources and simply could not fulfill the request. She answered, "I don't have any bread—only a handful of flour in a jar and a little oil in a jug. I'm gathering a few sticks to take home and make a meal for myself and my son, that we may eat it—and die."

Elijah first spoke to her fear of not having enough:

"Don't be afraid. Go home and do as you have said. But first make a small cake of bread for me from what you have and bring it to me and then make something for yourself and your son. For this is what

the Lord, the God of Israel says: 'The jar of flour will not be used up and the jug of oil will not run dry until the day the Lord gives rain on the land'"(1 Kings 17:13-15 NIV).

This bold widow took a leap of faith and obeyed the word of God and found out that she could trust His word. She took care of the man of God's need first—even before her own and her son's hunger—and God rewarded her by giving her an unending supply of oil and flour. They ate from that meal barrel for one year.

Elijah's principles of giving will work for you and me today:

1) Refuse the fear that says you will go without if you give.

2) Put God's needs before your own.

3) Step out by faith in obedience to what He told you to do.

Why would God ask a poor, starving widow to take care of someone else's need before her own? The same reason He asks us to support the missionary, feed an orphan, or supply Bibles in a foreign land…because He wants us to experience the kingdom of God advancing in the world through our personal lives. We are always the winner, never the loser, for following the formula for giving laid out in the Bible.

Did you notice that the prophet didn't ask the widow to feed the whole village…or build a church…or buy a new chariot for him? God always starts with what we have. For that widow at Zarephath, making one little bread-cake took all the faith she had, and that's what God wanted from her. He always sees quality, not quantity. God never judges us by another person's standards, just His own.

I know a man who on the fifteenth of each month emptied his bank account and gave it all to the Kingdom. He and his wife called it "zero-base-budgeting." Few people have that kind of faith, and I doubt that this couple started out with giving that much every month. But they learned that they can trust God and so they walked in an added grace of giving. Even though they emptied out their account every month, they added several rooms to their house and drove new automobiles.

God multiplies what we give Him, not what we hold on to. As we give what we have, God sees that we never lack. Just like the widow at Zarepath, we must keep moving forward in the grace of giving. When you lift up your offering to God, He reaches right back to you. But if you fold your arms, He can't get to your hands to fill them.

> *God multiplies what we give Him, not what we hold on to.*

One of the students at Christ for the Nations was barely "making ends meet" while she was going to school and paying off her tuition. One morning after I had taught on giving, she returned to her room and prayed, "Lord, I don't have anything to give. I have twenty-five cents to my name."

Her roommate needed a stamp for a letter to her parents, and so she gave her the last cents for the stamp. She left for her job, where she worked for an agnostic woman who ridiculed her for attending a Bible school. When she went to work that afternoon, she found her boss pacing the floor back and forth and thought something might be wrong.

"I don't understand this," she told her. "I think I'm supposed to give you fifty dollars."

Obviously, God wasn't being mean when He challenged this poor student to give her last twenty-five cents, just as Elijah wasn't being cruel when he asked the widow to make her last cake for him.

Have you ever tried to give candy to a toddler? You want to give them candy but their chubby little hands can only hold three or four pieces and then they start dropping what you've given them. You have a whole bag full of candy, but the problem is they can't contain all you want to give them.

God feels that way about you and me. He has so much to give us that our small hands and limited minds can't contain it all. God's not cheap and God's not stingy—He is a Giver. I've never heard of anyone going without what they needed because they gave. Obviously, the Psalmist David hasn't either: *"I have been young, and now am old; yet have I not seen the righteous forsaken nor his seed begging bread"* (Psalms 37:25 KJV).

If God's nature flows in us, we will constantly be growing in this grace of giving until it is a natural, joyful lifestyle and not a chore.

Giving is like everything else in our life. We start out with where we are and what we can give and God grows us through the seed we plant.

A Spoon and a Shovel:
How God Measures

5

Prosperity is not measured by what
you have but by what you give.

*"God's gifts are never loans; they are
always deposits."*

The Christians in Tepeapulco, Hidalgo, Mexico had one of those problems that every pastor hopes for: the church had grown so much they needed a larger building. In order to avoid the red tape involved in getting another building permit from the government, they simply put new walls around the original church. Their plan was simple—when they put the new roof on, they would tear down the inside building.

The problem was the roof. These Christians had used all of their faith and funds to get the walls up. How could they put on the roof—the most expensive part of the building—without funds?

"Brother Myers, I know that God uses you to inspire faith for finances," the pastor wrote me. "Would you come and minister at our church?"

I gladly agreed and drove the three hours from Mexico City, anticipating ministering to the people and raising the funds for the church roof. I had seen it happen all over Mexico and had no doubt that God would do it again in Tepeapulco.

That is, until I arrived.

I drove over to the pastor's home before the evening service. "Brother Myers, thank you for coming," he greeted me. "But I need to tell you that we have no money at all. We just bought musical instruments for the church orchestra, and the entire congregation has used all its resources. I'm sorry, but I don't think there's anything you can do for us tonight."

I excused myself and went to the church to pray. "Lord, I drove three hours to help these people," I began my complaint. "Have I wasted my time?" I was disgusted and discouraged and obviously in no frame of mind to preach a message on faith. My own had hit bottom. "Lord, is what this pastor said true? Is there no reason for me to be here tonight?"

"On the one hand, he told you the unadulterated truth," I heard God speaking into my spirit. "There are no finances. But on the other hand, he didn't tell you all the truth. At their present level of faith, there are no funds. That's why I sent you, son. Build their faith in My word and My word will lift their faith to another level. At that level there will be funds to roof this building."

I was energized to preach. I had heard from God and received my assignment for the evening's service. I had preached this message on faith and giving countless times and knew the scriptures and illustrations. But evidently I had not received all of my instructions.

"I want you to take a spoon and shovel to church tonight." I knew it was the voice of God still speaking into my spirit.

Now this was strange. I certainly didn't plan to eat. And of course I was not going to be digging either. Just as I offered the question that was forming in my mind to God, I thought of Luke 6:38. I had quoted the Scripture numerous times before, and knew it by heart:

"Give, and it will be given to you: good measure, pressed down, shaken together, and running over will be put into your bosom. For with the same measure that you use, it will be measured back to you."

GOD'S MEASUREMENTS

I could see God's purpose. The spoon and the shovel were measurements and a perfect illustration for those dear Mexican Christians who used both in their daily lives. In fact, I could get a spoon and a shovel for the evening message by simply walking back to the pastor's house.

I was amazed at how powerful the Word of God is. Minutes

before I was discouraged, thinking I had wasted my time by coming. Now, with the inspiration of the Holy Spirit and clear directions from God, I anticipated building the faith of the congregation.

That night we had a packed house but I didn't preach on giving. I knew that many were there who didn't know Jesus Christ, so I preached the message of the Cross and invited unbelievers to repent of their sins and start life over with Jesus.

Now it was time for the challenge. I read the verse in Luke 6:38 KJV:

"Give, and it shall be given unto you; good measure, pressed down, shaken together, and running over, shall men give unto your bosom."

I had asked the pastor for a large sack of beans and a washbasin. After I read the scripture in Luke, I put the washbasin on the table and filled it with beans, the staple of every Mexican's diet. I had their attention. From the back of the church, people perched on the edge of seats, straining to see this strange scene. Others giggled. *Had Hermano Myers lost his mind?*

"Is this good measure?" I asked the congregation.

"Si!" they shouted back.

Then I pressed it down, shook it, and began to pour more beans in the basin until it overflowed. Black beans spilled over the cement floor, the altar, and even over the little children who were sleeping near the altar. I continued to pour.

"Is this how you want to receive from God?" I asked again.

"Si, si," they started shouting. You could feel the mounting excitement as they began to understand the message of Luke 6:38.

I read the remainder of the text: *"For with the same measure that you use, it will be measured back to you"* (Luke 6:38 NKJV).

This time I picked up the teaspoon and put a few beans into it and held it up for the congregation to see. "Some people give their offerings to God with a teaspoon. When there is no work, the pantry is bare, and the children need school clothes, they begin to pray, 'Lord, meet my need!'"

"Of course I will," He responds. "I only have one request—may I borrow your teaspoon?"

"Oh no, Lord," we cry. "A teaspoon won't help me." And yet that is the measure we often use to give to the Lord. Do you think for a moment that God will violate the principle of His eternal Word? He won't rewrite the Book for us. When we use a teaspoon with Him, He has no choice but to bless us in "the same measure" without violating divine principles.

I reached for the shovel again. "Is this a measure?" I asked the congregation. Before they could answer, I filled it up with beans and challenged them with one more question: "How many want a shovelful?"

We raised the funds for the new roof that night. That church building is one of the prettiest churches in Mexico.

"In the same measure" is a truth that has been burned into my heart ever since that meeting in Tepeapulco. All of us want God to bless us. We pray and ask Him to enlarge us in our finances, to bless our relationships, and to stretch our borders.

"How much is a shovelful?" many people ask. "How much should I give?"

I refer them to John where Jesus uses the small lunch of a little boy to feed five thousand people. Those five little barley loaves and two small fish that he gave to the Lord were all he had—a shovelful.

Jesus commended the offering of a poor widow who dropped two copper coins into the offering basket at the temple because He knew it was a shovelful for her. In fact, it was all she had. Compared to her offering, the rich, throwing in their gold, only gave a teaspoonful. They gave only a small portion of their wealth. The widow gave all she had.

I have said it before, but it's worth repeating: God sees quality before He sees quantity. The quality of the gift determines the quality of the giver.

Isaac Manzano, a pastor from Necaxa, Mexico, told me about the time when eight Totonac Indian pastors unexpectedly showed up at his house. They arrived just before breakfast one morning after a grueling four-hour walk through the mountains. All of them were hungry and Pastor Manzano knew they needed a hearty breakfast. The problem was that he and his wife lived on a meager budget and had just enough money to buy sixteen eggs from the corner store.

> *God sees quality before He sees quantity. The quality of the gift determines the quality of the giver.*

"Honey, you don't get an egg this morning because there are eight men who have been walking and will eat at least two eggs per person," his wife told him.

The pastor understood. He and his family were used to putting the needs of their people before their own. But when his wife cracked opened the first egg, two yolks plopped into the dish.

"It looks like you get to eat!" she told her husband. She broke open the second egg and two yolks dropped into the dish again. "Look!" she told her husband, "there's enough for me." Each time she cracked one of those sixteen eggs, two yolks dropped into the dish.

After their guests left, Pastor Manzano hurried back to the market with borrowed money. He had come upon a way to stretch his pesos. He would simply buy more of those "miracle eggs."

"I want thirty-two of the exact same kind of eggs you sold me this morning," he instructed the woman behind the egg stall. She dutifully picked out thirty-two eggs from the same basket she had sold from earlier. Thinking he had just bought sixty-four eggs for the price of thirty-two, Manzano took the eggs back to his wife, sure he had found a way to save money.

When she cracked open the first egg, only one yolk fell out. Again and again, they cracked their eggs, but there was not a double-yolked egg in all of the thirty-two they had bought.

It was obvious that the reason God had given them double-yolked eggs was to meet the need of the morning breakfast. It may not have been as dramatic as the barley loaves and fish of a little boy to feed the five thousand. But no one could convince that couple that God had not multiplied egg yolks to feed eight hungry Indian pastors.

God delights in blessing sacrificial gifts. God uses different measures than we do. Little becomes much if He is in it, and on the other hand, much is little, if given selfishly. These truths exclude no one.

Money is not basically our problem. Our problem is the heart. When we love God more than we love things, then we will automatically lay all we have on the altar. How much do you want to receive from God? *God determines the size of our gift in proportion to the sacrifice that accompanies it.*

S E E I N G   T H E   6   I N V I S I B L E

Only those who see the invisible can
do the impossible.

*"You haven't begun to give until
you feel good about it."*

Once when I was asked to speak at a church conference on the subject of giving, I printed up hundreds of little red labels beforehand with one word stamped on them: *PERISHABLE.* After I spoke, I handed out those red labels to everyone at the conference, making sure they all got a handful of fifteen or twenty to take home with them.

"When you leave here, take these with you and use them," I instructed everyone. "Put one on the hood of your car because it's going to perish. Brand the door of your house with another one— it's going to perish, too. Stamp one on your bankbook because— you guessed it—it's going to perish." I challenged them to put it on their most prized antiques, their furniture, and their refrigerators.

Now I don't know if all those people went home and plastered red labels on their furniture, but that object lesson got my point across. We live in a perishable world, and yet most of us forget that fact. We live as if we were going to live for a thousand years down here. But no matter how well we take care of our bodies, they are perishable, too. Even if we could live that long, a thousand years are nothing compared to eternity.

No wonder Jesus commands us to develop a habit of looking at and living for the unseen: *"For the things which are seen are temporary, but the things which are not seen are eternal"* (2 Corinthians 4:18 NJKV).

Anything we can't relate to eternity is not worth our time. If money is our reason for living, then we have no reason to live. If our main goal on earth is not to seek God's kingdom, then we have no goals that are worth our time or effort. On the other hand, Jesus said that if we put His kingdom first in this world, then all these other things shall be added too. C.S. Lewis once said, "Aim at heaven and get the earth thrown in extra. Aim at the earth and you'll miss both." When you live to bless somebody else, you live in a dimension that is above the ordinary.

If you and I are going to leave an inheritance to God's work that can be transferred to the other side, then we must ask God to let us see the invisible. The faith that sees the invisible receives the incredible.

I was speaking at a large church in the city of Pachuca, Mexico, when a young Mexican man came up to me at the end of the service and asked if he could travel with me. "I'll carry your Bible and hand out flyers to advertise the meetings—whatever you need," he said. "I just want to learn how to do what you do."

His name was Jesus Castelazo, a poor, young minister with a wife and five children. I could see that he had a heart for God and told him that he was welcome to join me. I also told him it was important that he understand I was living by faith and could not promise him any financial support.

He agreed to step out by faith and we began traveling together, holding open-air meetings everywhere we went. True to his word, my new coworker helped me locate sites for new meetings, passed out handbills beforehand, and set up the P.A. system everywhere we went. He had only a third-grade education, but was highly intelligent and eager to learn. We studied the Bible together during the day and took turns preaching at night.

Castelazo became a valuable associate evangelist. When he told me the Lord was leading him to start a church in Tuxtla, the capital city of Chiapas, Martha and I gladly provided the fifty-six dollars a month to rent a place where he could launch his vision. They had found a house with a meeting room downstairs and living quarters for the family upstairs. It was perfect for their needs.

The location, however, was another matter altogether. They were in the middle of the city's red-light district. One square block housed nine bars and houses of prostitution. His neighbors were a street full of prostitutes and alcoholics. Two women witches lived next door.

"Brother Wayne, those women know enough obscenities to make an unregenerate sailor blush," he told me. "Even their two parrots are fluent in obscenities."

It was hardly a place where a young pastor would want to start a new church. But then, Castelazo was anything but typical.

After he moved his family into the upstairs living quarters of the building, Brother Castelazo bought the wood to build ten benches for his new church. He was determined to pray and to preach until the prostitutes (and men who came to visit them) were saved.

One day while working on the benches, with Mexican ranch music blaring from the bar across the street, he heard a voice taunting him: "What do you think you're doing building ten benches for a church? You don't even have a congregation."

Recognizing the enemy's voice, he immediately retaliated: "You're right, devil. I need twenty benches." He proceeded to build ten more wooden benches for a yet-to-be-born church.

Those twenty benches were not enough to accommodate the prostitutes and alcoholics who poured into the Castelazo's new church. Even the two witches who lived next door became born-again believers. When one of the madams who had owned several brothels gave her heart to the Lord and died a Christian, it impacted the whole neighborhood. The price of real estate went up because the area was no longer considered a "red-light district."

The most unusual testimony came from the parrots of the two former witches. "You won't believe this," Pastor Castelazo told me later, "but I was visiting those two women the other day and their foul-mouthed parrots began singing, *Hallelujah, Thine the Glory!*"

We helped that congregation build their first church which

seated several hundred. They soon grew so much they needed a larger building. Now we were raising funds for a church of two thousand. Through God's grace, Pastor Castelazo has built more than two hundred churches across Mexico and is now pastoring the nation's second largest evangelistic center with a seating capacity of eight thousand.

SEEING THE UNSEEN

Pastor Castelazo's vision that impacted the nation of Mexico began with his supernatural ability to see twenty benches filled with some of the world's most needy sinners. He discovered a truth that will work for you and me: we must see the invisible if we want to move into the realm of the supernatural.

When this truth takes possession of our heart, it will direct our hand to our pocketbook. When the heart is really converted, the pocket will be inverted. I've been in meetings where people have seen the invisible realm and have brought their cars, trucks, boats, guns, and even antiques to auction off for the purpose of furthering the gospel in the world. The proceeds were used to build churches or establish an orphanage or pay for a newly built Bible school.

> *We must see the invisible if we want to move into the realm of the supernatural.*

He is not rich that hoards much, but rather he that gives much. True riches are spiritual, but we can convert the temporal into the eternal if we labor every day to share our resources with those who are in need.

Jesus said in Matthew 6:21: *"where your treasure is there is your heart also.* "That simply means that if you value having a new car, a new house, or new possessions more than you value expanding the kingdom, you are making a statement about your eternal priorities. We only have in heaven what we deposit in that account while we are on earth. There's no way to transfer funds to heaven once we say good-bye to this world.

"If ye be risen with Christ, seek those things above," Paul admonishes us in Colossians 3:1. We do this by keeping our eyes focused on the God who promised to meet our needs, and the God who promised to use us in His kingdom. Jesus said, "As much as ye did it to the least of these—the hungry, the naked, the lame, the blind, the needy—you did it into Me." It takes supernatural eyesight to see Jesus when we see a beggar...or a single mother who can't pay her rent...or a missionary couple who need the funds to live in a third-world country. We extend the kingdom of God on earth when we live beyond the ordinary.

The servant of the great prophet Elisha learned this truth when an army of men was in hot pursuit of his master. He woke up early one morning to see horses and chariots surrounding the city and knew that Elisha and he were doomed. He did what you or I would have done in the same situation—he panicked.

"Oh my Lord, what shall we do?" he asked Elisha.

Elisha tried to reassure him with what seemed to be a ludicrous statement: "Those who are with us are more than those who are with them."

Elisha prayed a profound prayer for his servant that will still work today: *"O Lord, open his eyes so he may see"* (2 Kings 6:14–17).

Asking God to help us see what He alone sees will cause us to expend all we have for that unseen world where the price of a soul is worth more than the entire world (Mark 8:36-37).

Jesus revealed the desire of His heart when He asked us to pray that God would send out laborers into the harvest. But the lack of necessary resources is one of the great hindrances in expediting His prayer. In order to send forth workers, we must give of our finances. Partnering with the Castelazo's of the world—those who are willing to go and live among the most needy of sinners—is the only way to change the landscape of our global neighborhoods. The faith that enabled Pastor Castelazo to build twenty benches for a church in a red-light district and finally the largest church building in Mexico is the same faith you and I need to release our possessions. This kind of faith results in equipping ministers all over the world with the tools they need to get their job done.

O B E D I E N T G I V I N G

7

Failure in stewardship means
breakdown in fellowship.

*"God's supply is deposited all along
the road of obedience."*

One evening I was preaching in Mexico City in the home of Aurelio Arrache, one of my sons in the gospel. When I gave the altar call, a well-educated young man came forward to give his heart to the Lord. He introduced himself as Juan Manuel Nuñez. The following week he returned and received the baptism of the Holy Spirit. Not long afterwards, he began to work alongside a charismatic Catholic priest in his area, leading Catholic young people to the Lord.

When the priest was transferred, Juan Manuel began his own church. But before long he realized that something was missing. He had a heart for missions and knew God was calling him into one of the most challenging areas in all of Mexico—the state of San Luis Potosi. He targeted El Coyotc, a village about 400 miles north of Mexico City, and put down a stake for God in a barren, dry desert—both spiritually and physically.

Because there is little rainfall in that part of Mexico, the people there suffer from poor crops and little food. As a result of their abject poverty, many of the Mexicans in El Coyote make a living by catching snakes, birds and an occasional deer, then selling them alongside of the highway. The women sell themselves, offering their services to truck drivers driving through their area. Besides the poverty and prostitution, incest is rampant—not the kind of place a young minister would normally want to live, much less start a new church.

By that time, Juan Manuel had his own sons-in-the-gospel— Salvador Nuñez, a graduate from Christ for the Nations, and Octavio Flores. These two young men and their wives shared Juan Manuel's vision to see a church established in El Coyote. They began taking medical teams into that impoverished community, serving the physical needs of the people. Because these remarkable teams were willing to accept what could only be described as a "hardship tour of duty," a number of small congregations have been established in one of the most ungodly areas of Mexico.

I felt the Lord speak to me about buying a car for those two brave families. I responded by asking for His provision, "Lord, if these young families are willing to sacrifice their lives to plant churches in that barren, depraved area, then the least we can do is provide them with a truck that will make their job easier."

Several months later I was in Vancouver, Canada, speaking on missions when the pastor approached me. "Brother Wayne, you have raised money for our missionaries, but what about you? Do you have a need?"

I jumped at the opportunity to bless Salvador and Octavio: "I would like to put a new Nissan double-cab camper truck in the hands of two missionary couples working in one of the hardest areas in all of Mexico," I told him. He graciously agreed, and that night after my sermon, the Canadian brethren gave the needed funds for Salvador and Octavio's truck. Eight days later, the truck was purchased in Mexico City, loaded with supplies for the families, and sent down to El Coyote.

Another friend donated a used three and a half-ton Dodge truck for transporting clean water from as far as ten miles away. Since water is scarce, this gave them great favor in the communities and broke down suspicion. They had earned the respect of the people, which opened up the door for the gospel.

Juan Manuel established a church of 400 members in Mexico City, and founded numerous missions like El Coyote. Apart from his pioneer work, God has used him to start a family-counseling center in Cuernavaca, a city south of Mexico City with over half a million people.

OBEDIENCE AND FRUIT

I discovered a long time ago that if we want fruit that remains, we must learn to serve God with an obedient faith. Juan Manuel was born into the kingdom because of his obedient response to a word of salvation. His ministry was launched through the same obedience to the call of God to preach the gospel, and is still succeeding through obedience. When God told me to give a truck to help him in that ministry, my obedience was the opportunity for the Canadian brothers to obey the teaching they had just received on "Living to Give." The advance of the kingdom depends on all of us operating in an obedient faith.

Whether we like to admit it or not, little in the kingdom is accomplished without money. It takes money to send a missionary, feed the poor, buy a car for the nationals, or print the Bible in another language. It takes money to build our churches—both here and abroad. Serving the homeless and delivering the drug addict and prostitute from a lifestyle that is killing them requires finances.

Just because we are not called to live our life in a foreign land, does not mean that God does not expect us to be part of gathering in the harvest before Jesus returns to the earth.

I heard the story of a rich man who dreamed he was in heaven and Jesus showed him a great, numberless multitude.

"Look it over, my friend. How many are here because of you?"

The man looked and looked but couldn't see one face he recognized. When he woke up, he changed his life focus and became a soul winner.

In God's kingdom, our greatest joy will be to hear the Lord of the harvest say, "Your investment in a ministry...or your buying

Bibles...or your financing a vehicle, has brought many into the kingdom. Well done."

To have a part in this harvest of souls, you and I must practice an obedient faith that responds to whatever God tells us to do. *Obedient faith has to do with what we possess and comes from our known resources.* God speaks and says, "Give this piece of real estate to my kingdom for this new facility...or release that boat... or draw something out of your savings account."

> *If we only tithe ten percent after knowing God for ten years, we obviously have a lot of growing to do in the realm of stewardship.*

When some of us hear a word from God like that, fear grips our heart because we remember how long or how hard we worked for that real estate or boat or savings account. But fear will cause us to stagnate. Most Christians have grown in every area except giving. If we only tithe ten percent after knowing God for ten years, we obviously have a lot of growing to do in the realm of stewardship. Tithing is the beginning, where the children play, but should never be the conclusion of the matter.

OBEDIENCE EQUALS FAITH

Some of the most spontaneous, obedient acts of faith come from those who have very little of this world's goods. Once I was preaching in Mexico raising money for a church in Pachuca, in the state of Hidalgo. A ten-year-old girl said, "I don't have any money, but I have a piece of cloth worth fifteen pesos. I was going to make a new dress for Easter with this money, but I'll give it to the building fund."

Another woman said, "I make my living sewing, but I'll give my sewing machine motor to roof the church."

They were giving what they had.

I couldn't forget the offering of the girl who gave up her Easter dress so her city could have a church. Months later, when I returned to visit the church, I asked where she was. I knew God was not going to ignore a simple, precious faith like hers. I wanted to hear the rest of the story.

She approached me with a big smile on her face and said, "You know, I gave a piece of cloth worth fifteen pesos, and my brother gave me a beautiful piece of cloth and a brand new pair of shoes to match."

That's God. Don't try to rationalize God. You never know what He will do through your life or mine until we move into this realm of faith. When God speaks and we obey, we're acting out our faith. As you hear God's voice and act accordingly, He will show you how big He is. This is a faith that makes life interesting, rewarding, and abundant. It's not how much you have in your hand; it's how much God gives through it.

AUSSIE MIRACLES

I was in Australia in 1994, preaching in a small church of 150 adults and it happened to be Missions Sunday—a perfect opportunity to challenge the believers there to give. I spoke to them about faith-giving in the morning service. The small congregation wrote their faith commitments down on pieces of paper and dropped them in the offering plate.

That afternoon, I asked the pastor if he had any special mission projects that we could encourage the people to give to by making verbal faith promises.

"We owe 10,400 Australian dollars on a vehicle we're buying for a missionary family in Indonesia," he said. That's all I needed to know. I immediately began to target my faith for that $10,400 to send to Indonesia.

Perhaps it was just as well that I didn't know that a gentleman was in the congregation that night who had left the morning service angry with me. "The message is too mercenary," he told his pastor. He had decided that he would not give to the project and did not plan to return to the evening service.

"I want you to go back to the service tonight," the Holy Spirit spoke to his heart. "I have something to teach you."

That evening, I preached again on giving. After the sermon, I presented the challenge of the $10,400 needed to purchase the vehicle. I urged the congregation to step out by faith in obedience to the Word and make a financial commitment to purchase the car.

A man stood up in the back of the church and said, "I will pay for the car." The congregation turned around to see who was speaking. It was the brother who had been angry at my morning message. Even more startling—he was self-employed and business had been poor—so poor that he was without work.

A month later, I received a letter from Pastor Dunk telling me about two miracles that happened after I left their church. "One man wrote his faith commitment on a piece of paper in the morning service—even though he worked on commission and had not made any profit for five or six months. Two days after he submitted the faith promise, he sold over a million dollars worth of contracts."

The second miracle concerned the man who was angry at the message on giving but ended up making a faith promise of $10,400 to pay off the car for the missionaries. He had not eaten for three days because there was no food in his house. After he made the faith promise, he got a call from the Australian government informing him that he had been underpaid for a major project he had completed months before. Within thirty days, the government gave him enough money to pay off what he promised for the car, plus pay off $52,000 in debts that he owed.

"The spirit of mammon over my congregation was broken," Pastor Dunk reported. "Both joy and giving have increased in our church."

Our joy is in proportion to our obedience. If you haven't been blessed in sharing something, then ask God to help you step out and give in obedience to His Word. It's more blessed to share and to bless than it is to keep and to hold. I tell people, "You can't eat a 100-dollar bill—even the new ones don't have any flavor. You can salt and pepper it, add some mustard and mayonnaise, but it would still be hard to digest. On the other hand, if you take $100 and bless somebody else, it not only gives you a delicious satisfaction and joy in sharing, but it gives you fruit in eternity."

LIVING AND GIVING
THROUGH 8 FAITH

Faith is dead to doubts, dumb
to discouragement, blind to
impossibilities, and knows
nothing but success.

*"When the heart is converted, the
purse will be inverted."*

The Mexicans are a festive people who love to have fun and don't need a reason to have a party—just a pretext for one. They are family-oriented and turn events into full-fledged celebrations with minimum effort. Birthdays, weddings, anniversaries, promotions—all can be made into a major event. Good food and a mariachi band—a group of musicians singing Mexican folk music with the accompaniment of guitars, trumpets, accordions—provide the atmosphere for a jovial party.

Christians have often used these celebrations as evangelistic outreaches by inviting the villagers to come share a special dinner before a revival meeting. Many souls have entered the kingdom around a table laden with homemade tortillas, beans, and mole—a mouth-watering chili sauce made up of twenty-five different delicious ingredients.

Near Matamoros, a village south of Mexico City, one church celebrated its anniversary for three days. They invited believers and unbelievers from the nearby villages, and a guest minister to speak at their evening services. It was a great opportunity to reach out to those who were not Christians, as everyone in Mexico—saint and sinner alike—loves a celebration.

There was only one problem. Hosting a celebration of that magnitude required food—lots of it. When they tallied up the cost of feeding everyone for three days, the church elders realized they would need a miracle. How could a small village church feed so many people?

A woman stepped forward to supply all the chili peppers for the hot sauce. Another woman promised a three-day supply of beans. One man said he would provide the corn for the tortillas. Now all they lacked was the beef to make the tacos. But it was also the most expensive item on the list. No individual could afford three days' worth of meat to feed so many people. A silence fell over the group, killing the excitement and most of their faith. How were they going to find enough meat for the anniversary celebration?

"I'll bring the meat," said a brother from the back of the room. When they turned to see who had offered this generous gift, they were shocked that the voice belonged to Alberto, the poorest man in the church. He could hardly feed his own family and here he was offering to supply the most expensive item for the three-day meeting.

"Where are you going to get the meat?" the people wanted to know. "You don't even have a goat."

"I'll bring the meat," he said firmly.

Of course no one could rest until they knew how their poorest brother was planning to get the meat. They called another meeting and asked him when they could expect the meat, hoping he was going to explain his plan or back out of his promise.

"When do you need it?" he asked

"The day after tomorrow," they replied. We'll have to prepare our first breakfast at 6 A.M., and we will need the meat by then."

"All right, I'll have the meat to you by 6 A.M. but I will need six strong men and plenty of rope at my house by 4 A.M. tomorrow."

Six men volunteered, but they were still scratching their heads in bewilderment. Was the man not only poor but crazy, too? What if they started this meeting and humiliated themselves in front of the whole village?

On the morning of the first day of the meeting, six strong men with plenty of rope showed up at this Christian brother's house at 4 A.M. and found him waiting for them with an old battered rifle resting on his shoulder.

"Follow me," he said. "We're going hunting."

"And what will we hunt?" the men asked incredulously.

"Deer," he replied.

"We haven't had deer in this area for fifteen years," they scoffed.

Alberto started down the path. "Just follow me," he called over his shoulder. The men shrugged and set out with Brother Alberto, who began to praise God out loud for deer-meat tacos. They grumbled, but continued to follow close behind. At dawn, a buck junped in front of them. Alberto, still praising God, said, "Lord, you aim the gun and I'll pull the trigger."

One bullet dropped the animal. Amazed, three of the men tied it with a rope to drag it home. Ahead, another buck, larger than his brother, stepped out on the path. After Alberto shot it, he turned around and calmly asked, "By the way, men, how many more do you want?"

Alberto knew what you and I sometimes forget—God owns all the cattle on a thousand hills. Everything we need is available through the currency of faith. If we are to be givers—people who are always looking for ways to invest in the kingdom—we must also have faith in God's ability to supply what we don't have.

"This is the victory that overcomes the world, even our faith" (1 John 5:4). We were brought into the kingdom by faith and we need faith to make it to the end. From the new birth to heaven's portals, it's a continual faith walk. We're saved by faith, kept by faith, healed by faith. Faith produces the answers to our prayers and is the link between our petition and God's answer. According to Hebrews 11:6, we can't please God without faith. Faith from a pure heart with right motives will always be the greatest force in the universe.

FAITH TAKES RISKS

Faith that costs nothing and risks nothing is worth nothing. If you try to always play it safe, if you're afraid God is going to let you paint yourself into a corner, you will never see God's miracle-working power for you personally. There's an element of risk in faith. If we're not growing by stretching our boundaries, we're backing up and shriveling because faith has to be exercised to grow. Alberto took a risk when he invited six men to follow him to his miracle buck, but it was nothing compared to Abraham taking his son into the thicket and depending on God to supply a ram for him. The life of his son was at stake. Sometimes we never know what God can do until we are desperate for a miracle and move into this realm of faith because of our great need.

FAITH ALWAYS RELEASES

Abraham had such complete trust in God that He could agree to release the one dearest to his heart. When he took his son to the altar, he was living out a faith that taught him that he could give everything away and not lose. If God is stretching you in the area of finances, He may be asking you to trust Him enough to know you will never go without if you give away what you need. The more you have to give away, the more prayer it takes to wisely give it.

FAITH RECEIVES THE IMPOSSIBLE

God promised Abraham a son when he was almost 100 years old and when his wife was ninety. Yet in Romans, the Bible says that Abraham held strong in spite of the circumstances. Every day he waited, his faith got stronger, not weaker, and he expected Sarah to get pregnant. It was impossible for that couple to have a child, and yet Abraham and Sarah received the incredible.

> *If you want God to do something that He's never done for you before, then do something for God that you've never done before.*

Faith is dead to doubts, blind to impossibilities, dumb to discouragement, and sees nothing but success.

You don't need a great faith. You just need faith in a great God. If you face a mountain you can't climb over and you can't tunnel through, then turn it into a gold mine. Let me encourage you to stop telling God how big your mountain is, and start telling your mountain how big your God is.

Believe God to take the circumstances you can't change, and glorify Himself through His provision that He supplies.

Above all, don't give up—quitters lose all and winners take all. God is a supernatural God and it's natural for a supernatural God to have children who live supernaturally. Live expecting God to do the unexpected—to do things for you that He has never done before.

If you want God to do something that He's never done for you before, then do something for God that you've never done before.

He is not rich who saves much,
but rather he who gives much.

*"He who wants little
always has enough."*

When Martha and I think back on our first flight to Mozam-bique, we ask ourselves why we weren't frightened to fly in an old Italian Piaggio P 149 D-military trainer that had flown just four hours in the past eighteen years. It could be that our decision was influenced by the choice of four hours of flying time, or eleven hours in a truck on non-existent roads through bandit-infested bush. Whatever the reason, we climbed into the cockpit of the worn-out plane and discovered that the rear seating was a wooden bench. We learned that the Italian trainer plane had recently been rebuilt and this four-hour flight would determine if everything was working well.

Evidently not. When we approached the runway in Beira, Mozambique, a seaport city on the Indian Ocean, the landing-wheels would not descend. Rod Hein, our pilot, grabbed the manual lever but the safety catch cracked, snapped off, and lay swinging loosely in his hand. He managed to crank the wheels down manually before we dropped onto the runway. We were relieved to be on solid ground.

Not long after that flight, Rod took the Piaggio in for a mechanical check and was told by the airplane mechanic that the support structure in one of the wings was rusted. The plane was not air worthy. I was glad we didn't know that before our flight. Sometimes faith works better without all the facts!

Rod and Ellie Hein are two of the most committed, quality servants of God I have met anywhere in my life. We were honored by their invitation to visit them at their home in Zimbabwe to see first hand how God has used their lives to impact nations.

Ellie is fourth-generation European Zimbabwean whose father was murdered by terrorists. Their family has lived with the terrors of war and risked their lives to operate a famine and emergency relief program for their starving neighbors across the border in Mozambique. Besides establishing a Bible school in Inhaminga, Mozambique, God has used Rod and Ellie in an intricate role of finalizing the 1992 Peace Accord for Mozambique. They are two of the best reasons I know why we need to constantly give to the cause of Christ around the world.

After seeing the tremendous work for God that the Heins were doing, Martha and I wanted to financially partner with them by providing more reliable equipment for their work. I made a long distance call to the Heins and asked them how we could bless them.

"We desperately need a plane," Ellie told me over the phone. I knew this family had to have an airplane to get around in that African bush, just like I needed a car to maneuver the roads of Mexico. We committed ourselves to believe God to supply the first $20,000 toward a new plane. We told God that we were volunteering our services for Him to use us to raise the needed purchase price.

It was exciting to watch the body of Christ rally around a ministry in Mozambique they had never seen. I shared the Heins' need with several churches in Maryland and Delaware and they gave $18,000. When our dear friends in Mexico City, Gabriel and Lourdes Acero, pastors of Centro Cristiano Las Lomas, led their people in giving another $18,000 I felt tremendous pride in my dear Mexican brothers. They proved that they were second to none in giving for the cause of world missions.

Steve and Betty Bishop, friends who later visited the Hein family in Zimbabwe, shared our urgency to purchase the plane. They arranged a house meeting in Bedford, Texas, to share the need with thirty Spirit-filled Methodist couples.

At that time, Rod and Ellie were in the States and planned to share their need with the Bedford couples, but tragedy struck their family a few weeks before the meeting. Dustin, their only son, twenty-one years old, was killed back in Africa while flying an Ultra Light in the desert.

Rod and Ellie were determined not to give up their call to Mozambique—even though they were in deep grief over their son's death. I offered to attend the house meeting in their stead. I knew we must not give up our efforts to provide the best airplane possible for this family.

The night of the meeting, our hearts heavy with sorrow for Rod and Ellie's loss, Martha and I drove to Bedford. The weather was dark and foreboding and a tornado watch was out for the area. Only half of the thirty couples showed up.

"Lord, I will do my best to encourage these people to be a part of the African harvest," I prayed. "I refuse to be discouraged by the weather or by the fact that there are only fifteen couples instead of thirty."

During the meeting, I shared with the group how Rod and Ellie were impacting the nations of Zimbabwe and Mozambique. I asked these faithful believers to join with me in making financial promises by faith to broaden their vision.

There was no begging or pleading—just a simple presentation of the facts of the Word of God and the Heins' need. In less than fifteen minutes, those couples gave $75,000 in faith promises. Every penny of the faith promises came in. The Hein family is still flying the six-seater Cessna 206 purchased in South Africa with the $132,000 that was raised. That is the power of corporate faith promises.

It Takes a Community

Could one person buy a $132,000 airplane? Although there are those individuals who are able to write out such a check, usually it takes a community of believers working together to see great things done for God's glory. Raising the money needed for the Heins' airplane was a great miracle. The second miracle was watching Christians link hands from Texas to Maryland to Mexico and England, working for a common goal without knowing one another.

I thank God for the denominational sending organizations that have the means to finance schools, hospitals, and churches. They are doing a great work. However, many missionaries, from America and other countries, are independent and come from small independent churches. Who do they depend on to help them with finances? There are thousands of laborers in the field like Rod and Ellie Hein who need equipment and yet have no large organization underwriting their needs.

By God's grace, churches have been built around the world where the resources in one village of poor believers are inadequate to complete the building. They lay the foundation and build the walls, assisted by our partnership with Christ for the Nations, individual churches, friends, and supporters who fund the materials for the roof. This partnership enables many to share in the harvest.

Making a faith commitment allows us to join hands together in a spirit that says, "Let's get the job done...here's what I have. What can you do?" By creating a team spirit, we can see goals met that would be impossible for the average church member to accomplish on their own.

JOINT OWNERSHIP

The link between the giver and the recipient of a faith promise gift is a force that changes both the local church and the work of God in a foreign country. Solomon wisely said that two are stronger than one and a three-fold cord is not easily broken. In corporate faith promises, we form an invincible army in promoting the advance of God's kingdom among men.

> *The link between the giver and the recipient of a faith promise gift is a force that changes both the local church and the work of God in a foreign country.*

When we build a church, support an orphan, or build a Bible school, our offering binds us together with the global body of believers. Many times our initial offering initiates a life-long friendship and mutual prayer support between the giver and the recipient. We all tend to pray for the people we give to—it's a proven fact that when we give our money we make a heart commitment. *"Where your treasure is, there also is your heart"* (Matthew 6:21).

Through faith promises we are presented an opportunity to get involved and take ownership of our church's vision. The pastor is not left to shoulder the financial burdens alone. Everyone has an opportunity to be connected above their regular tithes, in proportion to their present resources and creative faith. When church members make a faith promise to help their pastor build a church, they are investing more than their money; they are signing up to be a part of the success of the local body.

I'm aware that many people do not believe in making faith

promises, but I have never made an apology for what I see as a scriptural principle. I have spoken in multiple mission conferences from Europe to Australia and across America, Mexico, South America, and Canada and watched God's people give millions of dollars for the gospel's sake. Every dollar we have raised goes through the local church—not my own association. When I teach on giving through making faith promises, I often lead the people and set the example by giving to their missionaries first. My faith has been stretched right along with everyone else's to believe God to supply the need to fulfill my promise on time. He has never let me down.

Sometimes I hear people say, "I don't like to make promises to God. It's a very serious matter and I might not be able to pay it." And yet they made a promise to the Ford Company, to Penney's, and to Sears. It is strange to me that people will go into debt to man but are afraid to make a commitment to God. God is a lot more lenient than the Ford Company—if you don't make the payment, your car will be repossessed. On the other hand, I've never yet heard of a church or pastor that refuses fellowship to a member who is struggling to pay a faith promise.

PRIVATE AND PUBLIC GIVING

Do public faith promises promote pride? The argument is sometimes used that Jesus admonished us not to be like the hypocrites who gave to be seen in public. I agree that giving should never be done with the motive of pride. Martha and I give most of our gifts privately, just as I do most of my praying in private. I counsel those who have misinterpreted that verse to read further and notice that Jesus also says that when we pray, we should go into the closet and shut the door behind us (Matthew 6:3-6). Does this mean that we should never pray in public? Consistency demands that we follow through on both verses in the same manner.

In Matthew 6:3-6, Jesus warned us to avoid a hypocritical, proud spirit in giving and praying. However, that is not cause to quit giving or praying publicly. Zacchaeus gave half his income publicly and there is no record of Jesus admonishing him to be quiet.

"But Zacchaeus stood up and said to the Lord, 'Look, Lord! Here and now I give half of my possessions to the poor...'

"Jesus said to him, 'Today salvation has come to this house, because this man, too, is a son of Abraham'." (Luke 19:8-9 NIV)

NOISY OFFERINGS

I once ministered to two hundred Christians in the mountains of San Luis Potosi, Mexico, six hours by mule from the nearest road. The believers there desperately needed a church building, as their present one—made of adobe with a thatched roof—was inadequate for their growing congregation. These Indian believers were poor. They lived in pole stick huts with thatched roofs. The women cooked outside on the ground with three rocks for a stove. A working man in that village earned $3.00 a day.

I challenged them to give, despite their poverty, and their response was immediate. Many women gave chickens and an occasional pig, which was a great sacrifice. Chickens were expensive, but giving a pig was equal to giving away the family savings.

While I was preaching, one man left the service and went home. When he returned he was leading a full-grown bull, his gift to the building fund. There was no way for the cackling hen or the squealing pig or the bellowing bull to be a secret offering. That's all they had.

In the early church, giving was done both publicly and corporately:

"No one claimed that any of his possessions was his own, but they shared everything they had....There were no needy persons among them. For from time to time those who owned lands or houses sold them, brought the money from the sales and put it at the apostles' feet, and it was distributed to everyone as he had need" (Acts 4:32-34 NIV).

GIVING IN A SPIRIT OF LOVE

The church has suffered much shame in the area of giving because of greed and misused funds. But just because the words *love* and *faith* have been abused and misused, this does not nullify the fact that love is the door and faith is the key to the storehouse of God—"The only thing that counts is faith expressing itself in love" (Galatians 5:6). *I have found that sincere hearts never confuse giving motivated by divine love with the emotional manipulation of men.*

John Maxwell, the well-known speaker and author, was once raising money to build a church he pastored. One church member, a widow living in government housing, gave an envelope with $3.47.

"I can't take that," the pastor told the poor widow.

"I'm not giving it to you," was her reply. "I'm giving it to God."

When Pastor Maxwell mentioned the widow's gift in a service, one of the men of his congregation stood up and said, "I'll give you ten dollars for one of those pennies."

When he sat down, another man offered to buy another one of the pennies. A penny auction started right there in the meeting, with church members buying every one of the 347 cents the widow had given. In the end, that small offering ended up bringing in over $3,300.

Obviously, that poor widow was not giving for show, but humbly, out of her poverty. Her act ignited a spirit of giving in the church that amounted to much more than she could have given on her own.

BUILDING TOGETHER

Corporate public giving does not need to be hypocritical, proud, or manipulative. Rather, believers who willingly join faith and finances to build the kingdom of God discover the creative power of unity. Anything is possible when we *give together* with a spirit of faith and love.

Feed your faith and your doubts
will die of starvation.

*"When a man prospers, God
either gains a partner or
Satan gains a fool."*

The first time I met Grant and Phillipa Gill was in England at Reinhard Bonnke's Fire Conference in the city of Birmingham. Brother Bonnke had asked me to join his team for the outreach into that city and to teach workshops on *Living to Give*. At his request, Martha and I flew to England several weeks before the meeting, to challenge local churches in the area to join in the work and expenses of the campaign.

The Gills, we discovered, were from South Africa and were also on the Fire Conference team. Grant graciously offered to be our guide to the city during the day and drive us to various churches in the evening. By the beginning of the Reinhard conference, he had listened to my message on giving so often he could have preached my sermons himself.

I ran into Grant and Phillipa twelve years later on another visit to England and found them pastoring their own church in the city of Chatman. I knew immediately that Grant was a man with a heart for God who loved to give. He told me about the time he invited the whole city of Chatman to a barbeque dinner as guests of his church. He ended up feeding 4,000 guests in that outreach, but for some reason the local pastors were not pleased. One of the pastors accused Grant of being overly generous—a badge of honor as far as I'm concerned.

He explained that after the Fire Conference he returned to South Africa and asked God to help him put the messages he had heard on giving into practice. Grant set a giving goal and prayed for faith to reach it. Later, he confessed, that he had asked God "for the same kind of faith as Wayne Myers has to believe for the money to buy a vehicle for a missionary."

The next day, he went to a closed bid auction for cars,

anticipating that God would lead him to buy the right one. Just to make sure that he would get the bid on one of the vehicles before the day was out, he bid on all eleven cars. He reasoned that one of them would be the right price.

He waited until the end of the day for all the bids to be reviewed to see if he had bought a car. When the new owners of the cars were finally announced, he was shocked to discover that his name was on all eleven cars.

"Dear God, what am I going to do?" he prayed. God and he both knew that he barely had enough money to purchase one car, much less eleven.

He went over to look at one of the cars, a Ford station wagon, and asked if he could test-drive it by himself. He needed to get alone to quiet his palpitating heart, and to ask God what he should do. He drove and prayed, asking God for direction. A few minutes later he saw a sign advertising, "Cash for Fords." He stopped and asked the owners how much they would give him for the Ford station wagon he was driving.

"13,500 rand," they told him. It just so happened 13,500 rand was the amount he needed to complete the purchase on all of the eleven cars he had bid on. He sold the Ford and gave ten vehicles away.

CREATIVE FAITH

I call this kind of giving creative faith and have seen it work multiple times all over the world. Creative faith is the kind of faith that believes God will go beyond what you think you can do and supply what you don't have. Martha and I give most of our offerings in this creative realm—we make a faith promise and God supplies the money to honor our commitment. We never send out a letter asking people to get us off the hook—it is a naked faith in a faithful God. Time and again we have witnessed miracles of God's timely provision. Creative giving does not come out of your budget but from God's limitless storehouse of supply.

Creative faith is the kind of faith that allowed the Corinthian church to give beyond what their natural circumstances dictated.

"Out of the most severe trial, their overflowing joy and their extreme poverty welled up in rich generosity. For I testify that they gave as much as they were able, and even beyond their ability" (2 Corinthians 8:2 NIV).

> *Creative faith is the kind of faith that believes God will go beyond what you think you can do and supply what you don't have.*

Giving "beyond our ability" propels us out of the comfort zone of what we can do into the impossible realm where we must believe God for the supply. Most of us don't start out at this place of giving. The starting point of operating in the creative faith realm is being generous with what God has already given you.

Years ago I took small, beginner steps in creative faith giving, and to this day, have never stopped asking God to challenge my faith and the amount that I give. One of those "beginner steps" of moving into a place of creative faith giving was when Martha and I were coming out of Mexico to visit my aging parents in Mississippi. David Nunn, a well-known evangelist, called me and said, "Wayne, we're having a convention of evangelists in Houston at the Hilton Hotel. If you come, I would love for you to share in our meetings."

Since Houston was enroute to Mississippi, we decided to stop at the conference. My problem was that I had given the last of our money toward a church construction project in Mexico. I had thirteen dollars in my pocket when I arrived in Houston— hardly enough to stay in the Hilton Hotel where the convention was being held. In those days, the hotel didn't require a credit card or cash in advance so I checked in, believing that God wanted me there and would provide for my expenses.

We arrived in time to join the evening service. When they passed the offering bucket, I threw in my last ten dollar bill. I could see no reason to prolong the inevitable if you only have a ten dollar bill between you and starvation. The moment I tossed the ten dollars in the offering, David Nunn saw me, called me to the platform, greeted me with a big hug, and pressed fifty dollars into my hand.

"Thank you, God," I prayed silently. I had walked out on the water of the impossible and He had met me.

The cost of our hotel room was eighteen dollars a night and we planned to be there for two nights—Sunday and Monday. But I gave an offering in every service and got up on Tuesday morning with twenty-one dollars left. I hadn't paid the hotel bill and felt the enemy putting fear into my heart, but I refused to be intimidated by doubt.

"Devil, come here. I have a word for you. I'm going to make you out a liar. I'm going to give away this twenty-one dollars. Only you and God and I are going to know about it. I want you to watch God get me out of this hotel with all bills paid."

I gave away another dollar and that left me with twenty dollars in my pocket. In the morning service I dropped my last twenty into the offering plate. I did it—I was now officially broke. I knew God was teaching me that He could take care of me. The meeting wasn't quite over when David Nunn walked into the service from the back of the building, came up behind me, and said, "Brother Wayne, I forgot to tell you that I'm picking up your hotel bill."

"Did you hear that, Satan?" I wanted to make sure he'd seen God come through for me.

In the afternoon meeting, Brother Nunn shared that he was going to Lima, Peru for a citywide evangelistic campaign there. When he asked who would like to give money toward the meeting, I raised my hand and made a promise for $100. My hand was still in the air when I heard the devil say, " Wayne Myers, you don't even have enough money to get to Mississippi and now you're making a commitment for a hundred dollars."

Just to make sure the enemy of my faith didn't win this battle, I spoke up, "Please increase my commitment to $200."

To my consternation, I learned that the offering was not a faith promise where you are given weeks or months to send in the money. Instead, the minister invited all those who had promised to give, to go into a back room together so the money could be collected.

I began to pray desperately, "O God, I made that promise in your name and we're both going to be embarrassed if you don't come through for me." I had believed God often to supply money needed in time frames of weeks and months, but never before had I been in a position of believing for a miracle in the amount of time it took to walk from my seat to a back room of an auditorium.

We sat down while people wrote out their checks and handed them to the ushers. Just before they approached me I recognized a voice behind me, "Do you have a bank draft? I'd like the privilege of paying Wayne Myers' $200 faith promise." It was our dear friend, Elizabeth Clark, a housewife who had been our family's personal intercessor for many years.

I was so relieved I could have shouted. *Did you hear that devil?* I was now $200 richer in the kingdom and my faith had been stretched to a new high in the process. I had entered the Hilton Hotel with a little over thirteen dollars in my pocket, had given in every offering, invested $200 in Peru, and was leaving with my hotel bill paid in full.

There was one problem. Martha and I didn't have enough money to buy gas to Mississippi. Martha emptied her purse—$3.67—just enough money to buy the gas to Beaumont, Texas.

A friend who needed a ride to Beaumont was in the back seat. She had no idea of the state of our financial condition or that she was literally riding on fumes of faith. Martha and I refused to even act like we needed gas money, much less speak about our need. Several miles down the road, our passenger casually remarked from the back seat, "Brother Wayne, I must be getting old. I've had a check made out to you for three weeks and never sent it to Mexico. I'll give it to you as soon as we get to my house." I didn't dare look at Martha for fear that we would both start shouting.

My relatives have seldom given to our ministry. They love us and were proud of what we were doing, but we never discussed our finances with them and they never felt impressed to systematically support us. But that trip was an exception. Before we left, my Dad pressed an offering into my hand, never knowing that he was taking part in the miracle of our day-by-day walk of faith.

I wouldn't take anything for those times when God stretched us out of the comfortable into the supernatural. Unless we are stretching, we are shrinking. After fifty-six years in the ministry, I still know that heart-palpitating, faith-stretching kind of experience waiting for God's miracle. The difference is that now instead of two or three hundred dollars, we expect thousands of dollars to advance the kingdom around the world.

If you have made a decision to grow in the grace of giving, God will honor your steps into the realm of reaching for the impossible.

> *I never grow in the grace of giving unless I take on a new challenge.*

Most Christians don't give much more than tithes—which belong to God anyway—but we should all be increasing the amount of money we give on a regular basis. I never receive more by giving less. There's a saying I believe: "when we store, we get no more." I have never advanced by backing up. I never grow in the grace of giving unless I take on a new challenge.

This is the only way we discover God's unlimited supply. When we start with what we have, we are laying the foundation to move into *creative giving*.

PRESUMPTUOUS GIVING

"Is it possible to be presumptuous in this faith giving?" people sometimes ask me. My answer is, "Yes, of course, it is possible."

A gentleman in one of our meetings once promised $100,000 toward a mission project and never paid one penny of it. Some time later, I ran into him and asked about the promise he had made. He admitted that he had given up on being able to pay the large amount.

"Even a dollar a month is better than disregarding your commitment altogether," I admonished him. We weren't concerned about the money—I knew from experience that God would supply what he wasn't able to give. Although there was no condemnation, integrity demands that we be accountable to our word in some way. I want to put as much emphasis on the validity of my word as God puts on His. If I don't, I've learned that I bring God's Word down to my own level of unfulfillment.

Please let me add that in every conference and church I have taught this message of giving, no one was coerced or intimidated to pay their faith promises. Giving is voluntary. The kind of gift that is a sweet-smelling savor to God. *"Entirely on their own, they urgently pleaded with us for the privilege of sharing in this service to the saints."* (2 Corinthians 8:3-4 NIV)

Those early saints are our examples—they saw giving as a privilege, not as drudgery. Even though they lived in extreme poverty, they begged Paul and the apostles to take their gifts.

How do you know that you are not giving presumptuously? Faith promises are usually made after our faith is built up through the Word of God. In response, we make a commitment that is born of faith and not just desire. This doesn't mean that you might not wake up at 3:00 A.M. wondering where the money is going to come from! Anything that propels us to our knees in a dependence on God is good for the soul.

THE BATTLE OF FAITH

Just like everything else you pray for in faith, the enemy will come to taunt you into believing you made a mistake in making a financial faith promise. That's when I give the devil a Bible study on his future from God's Word. Standing in faith for financial provision is no different from the faith we exercise when we pray for a healing or a family situation. *Many times there is no evidence that God has heard us, but we stand firm in our confidence in the Word of God.*

Desire plus faith minus unbelief equals the answer. If we could only see how big God is, we would not be afraid of being left stranded in our need. God wants us to reach beyond ourselves so He can meet us and take us to a higher level. The faith walk is similar to playing chess—it takes two to play. You move, God moves. God won't move for you and you can't move for God.

I preached recently at a church of 3,500 members in Cuidad Juarez, across the border from El Paso, Texas. The worship leader approached me after the service and reminded me of the time I had spoken in the same church fifteen years earlier.

"We were a small group of 250 members, meeting in the city library twice a week and you challenged us to buy our own property," he said. "I made a creative faith promise to give $2,000 U.S. dollars. Afterwards I wondered how I would ever come up with that extra amount in my budget."

"So, how did you do it?" I prodded him, knowing another testimony of a miracle was unfolding.

He told me how he worked in an auto parts company. After a week of wondering how he was going to pay his commitment, he finally picked up the phone to sell his automobile.

"I just didn't see any other way," he said. "But just as I picked up the phone I heard God say, 'Put the phone down. I don't want your car. I want to show you how big I am.' I knew it was the voice of God, so I obeyed and spent another week praying and asking God how He was going to provide for my $2,000 promise."

The next week his manager called him in and said, " You've made some excellent sales but we haven't paid you a commission." His boss gave him a check for exactly $2,000.

"Within fourteen months, I was making ten times as much as I did before I began to give by creative faith," he told me. He kept his car and his salary jumped higher, but the greatest increase was in the area of his faith. He is now in full-time ministry with a tremendous anointing for leading worship.

You are not limited to the balance in your checkbook. If you'll reach out with a pure motive, beyond what you think you can do God will reach down and show you His greatness. You see, you can't buy God's blessing, but through faith, you can open the door to heaven's storehouse.

Creative faith moves us into another dimension. It takes the wraps off God. When we declare that we are going to give beyond the possible, we are partnering with God. Churches are built, cars are given, national pastors are equipped, and Bibles are bought and distributed. This is the way we fulfill the desire of God's heart to reach the nations with the saving knowledge of His son, Jesus Christ.

11
GIVING WITH A WILLING HEART

God can only trust you with
funds when material things
become immaterial.

*"Give without remembering; receive
without forgetting."*

There was a Mexican man, a public accountant, who made good money in his profession. He heard the gospel and wanted to be a Christian, but under one condition.

"I want God to cleanse my filthy heart and put my name in the Lamb's Book of Life," he told the preacher, "but I want Him to keep His hands out of my pockets as long as I live."

Evidently he meant it. God mercifully saved him, but every time they passed the offering plate at church, he folded his arms and wore an expression of pure distaste. He looked like a man who had just taken a bath in lime juice.

One day he approached the pastor, his head bowed in humility, obviously convicted by the Holy Spirit for his attitude. "Pastor, I've got to pay my tithes. It's in the Bible. I want to pay my tithes for twelve months in advance."

Curious at this sudden change of heart, the pastor asked why he was choosing to pay all his tithes at once.

"I prefer one gigantic pain to twelve months of recurring discomfort," he replied.

The next week, his boss gave the accountant an unexpected raise. He returned to the pastor, this time with an automobile he had brought as a gift. He had become a giver as well as a tither.

I like this story because the man was honest—with himself, with his pastor, and with God. Many of us are not willing to admit that there are times we give while begrudging the loss to our budget and lifestyle.

GOD NEEDS GIVERS

Since the beginning, God's work has always required people to give in order to see God's plan accomplished on the earth. David knew God had chosen his son Solomon to build a great temple. David's part was to lay out the plans and provide the resources to get the job done.

Gold, silver, bronze, precious stones—the budget for this magnificent edifice was costly. David began gathering the priceless, but necessary, materials. Then he did something that every pastor and leader should take note of if they want a congregation of givers: David gave out of his private treasure.

"Moreover, because I have set my affection on the house of my God, in addition to all I have prepared for the holy house, I have a private treasure of gold and silver which I give for the house of my God" (1 Chronicles 29:3 AMPLIFIED).

Leaders and pastors should be the first to dip into their private bank accounts to meet the need of the house of God. Martha and I can testify that all over the world we have seen this principle work as we lead people in giving the "first fruits" of the offering. Whatever the local need may be—a church building, an automobile for a missionary family, or a Bible school in a foreign land—Martha and I usually make the first promise to meet that need. Not only have we reaped God's gracious blessings in our family, we have watched while a spirit of giving is released in congregations of every size.

GIVING WILLING OFFERINGS

After David laid his private bank account of silver and gold on the altar, he challenged his people with a pointed question: *"Now who will offer willingly to fill his hand [and consecrate it] today to the Lord"* (I Chronicles 29:5 AMPLIFIED).

It is interesting that David didn't just ask for an offering. He asked the people to give a willing offering. There is a difference. I challenge you to read this passage and to notice how often the words willingly, freely, voluntarily crop up. These words describe David's heart of worship:

"I know also, my God, that You try the heart and delight in uprightness. In the uprightness of my heart I have freely offered all these things. And now I have seen with joy Your people who are present here offer voluntarily and freely to You." (1 Chronicles 29:17 AMPLIFIED)

WHERE DOES OUR MONEY COME FROM?

The key to giving willing offerings to God is in the prayer David prayed after he collected his people's gifts for this great project:

"Yours O Lord, is the greatness and the power and the glory and the victory and the majesty, for all that is in the heavens and the earth is Yours; Yours is the kingdom, O Lord, and Yours it is to be exalted as Head over all. Both riches and honor come from You and You reign over all...." (1 Chronicles 29:11-12 AMPLIFIED).

David had a clear understanding that everything he had, indeed everything in the heavens and earth belonged to God (Haggai 2:8). Riches come from God. Everything we have is a gift from God.

When we walk in this understanding, we will gladly worship Him with what is in our hand.

When my son David was a small boy, he would sometimes dig into my pocket to find money to buy me a gift. We do the same thing when we give to God. We give back to Him what He gave us first. God wants us to see that we are only stewards and not owners.

GRATEFULNESS BEGETS GENEROSITY

Notice David's attitude of gratitude. "And now, O Lord, we give you thanks and praise your holy name" (1 Chronicles 29:13 AMPLIFIED).

While David offers his personal bank account to build God's temple, he stops to thank God for what He has been given. An attitude of gratefulness and thanksgiving will transform us into extravagant givers. Of all the people in the world, we western Christians have the most reasons to be grateful. The average annual income in many countries is $200. Compare that to our two-car garages, packed pantries, and recreational lifestyle and it becomes a little easier to remember why we should be grateful.

An Asian Christian remarked that the first thing he wanted to do when he arrived in heaven was to thank the Lord Jesus for loving him enough to save him. He continued, "Then I want to seek out the missionary that told me about Jesus." His final request was to be able "to go find all the people who supported the missionary and thank them for helping him proclaim the message of Jesus Christ to those who didn't know Him."

If we value the free gift of salvation, we will do everything we can to make sure this same salvation is made available to every nation, every tribe, and every tongue on earth.

We can learn to give happily to those in need. When we are always ready to share what God has given us, we store up treasures in heaven (Matthew 6:19-20). It is the only investment that is safe for all eternity.

> *If we value the free gift of salvation, we will do everything we can to make sure this same salvation is made available to every nation, every tribe, and every tongue on earth.*

GIVING WITH JOY

It is rare to find such generous, jubilant giving as I experienced in Hawaii, where I was one of the invited speakers for a conference. The church there needed a new building. While Randy White was preaching, the Christians brought personal belongings to the church until 3:00 A.M. Nineteen cars were donated toward the building fund and not one of them had been asked for. These were spontaneous acts of generous giving, prompted by a spirit of gratefulness.

God prizes cheerful givers. 2 Corinthians 9:7 NIV is a reminder that He takes no joy in a reluctant giver who gives under compulsion: "Each man should give what he has decided in his heart to give, not reluctantly or under compulsion, for God loves a cheerful giver."

THE REWARD

When David gave God his personal store of gold and silver, offering all he had on the altar for the purpose of fulfilling the dream of God's heart, God gave everything right back to David: *"Thus David, son of Jesse, reigned over all Israel...He died at a good old age...full and satisfied with days, riches and honor"* (1 Chronicles 29:28). While David only gave back the possessions that came from God Himself, God turned around and increased his riches. He also added honor and a long, satisfying life.

"A generous man will himself be blessed," Proverbs 22:9 NIV says. In other words, it is a law of God that everything you give away returns to you. While it should never be our motive to give in order to get, God makes sure we are rewarded for putting His kingdom first on earth. It is the law of sowing and reaping. It is the basic principle of Galatians 6:7: *"For whatever a man sows, that is what he will reap."* You can't sow into God's kingdom without reaping a harvest.

I've watched people grow in the grace of giving, stepping out further each time to give God more than before. And each time, they have discovered that God keeps increasing His blessing on their lives.

I remember a man in Mexico who promised 120,000 pesos towards the purchase of a church property. He was newly married and unemployed, so it was a step of faith. He told his wife, "We spend 1,000 pesos a day for food. Tomorrow, we will fast and pay the 1,000 pesos toward the 120,000 that we owe, so God will know we are serious about our promise." The next week he got a good paying job and was soon able to pay off the 120,000 pesos.

Several years later, he promised 300,000 pesos and gave it all. Then he promised one million pesos and paid that as well. Each time he trusted God to supply, and God kept increasing his finances. I have seen this happen over and over again.

God can take little and multiply it. It has been said, "Two plus two is four; two plus two—plus God—is more."

When people give out of their hearts, willingly and cheerfully, even though it's little, God delights to multiply it.

CHAPTER 12

GIVING GOD
SOMETHING PRECIOUS

God never asks for the lesser, but
for the precious.

*"Give, not from the top of your
purse but from the bottom
of your heart."*

I have always enjoyed teaching young people because they aren't bogged down in spiritual ruts, and they are often eager to practice what they have been taught. I often speak at *Christ for the Nations* (CFNI), a Bible college in Dallas, Texas, where I initiated a time I call, "Bless Another Week."

For years, CFNI students have practiced giving to missions, their churches, roommates, and friends during this special week of focusing on someone else's needs. I tell them that if they learn how to be givers at their age, their lives will never be boring because they will be a part of the great work that God is doing all over the world. I teach them to operate their finances with integrity and generosity so that God can use them and enlarge their ministries.

Most of these kids are working to pay their college expenses and have little spare change. In fact, the great majority pray they'll make it through the semester with all their bills paid on time. It sounds harsh to some, but we teach them to give anyway. Giving isn't limited to money, of course. I challenge them to give a special blouse a roommate has borrowed, or a tennis racket a friend has admired, or a free night of baby-sitting for a staff member.

I warn them, "Don't give something old and worn out." Give God something precious. Something that has value to you.

Every year, I watch some students struggle with my challenge at the beginning of the special-emphasis week. I can see the consternation they feel as they think of some of their favorite possessions. But by the end of the week, love conquers and you see roommates hugging and crying out their forgiveness and appreciation of each other.

Giving is healthy for relationships. How can you doubt someone's love when they take off their gold necklace and give it to you? Misunderstandings and hidden judgments are often healed in this flow of unselfish sharing.

Some students, owing on their school bill, will voluntarily pay for another student's tuition, or help buy a car for someone who needs transportation. Some walk to the accounting office and pay on their friend's tuition.

It feels like the school is celebrating Christmas in July. Actually, it's better than Christmas because no one expects a gift in return. It's all about blessing someone else. And of course, the blessing always returns to the giver. I cannot take credit for this "give God something precious" concept. It was not my idea. The principle is found in Mark 14, one of my favorite scripture passages. A woman who is courageous enough to interrupt Jesus' visit at the home of Simon, the leper, is deeply sensitive to the needs of her Master. No one but the Lord knew that she was actually anointing his body for burial.

> *Misunderstandings and hidden judgments are often healed in this flow of unselfish sharing.*

The gesture is one of costly worship bathed in the spirit of humility. She broke open her alabaster box of perfume—worth a year's wages—without regard of the profit she had lost by not selling it. She was oblivious to the judgments of others, including the "spiritual" disciples who dismissed her act as wasteful and foolish.

"But some were indignantly remarking to one another, 'Why has this perfume been wasted?'" (Mark 14:4).

The Bible says they were actually scolding her: "For this perfume might have been sold for over three hundred denarii, and the money given to the poor." Imagine them watching this beautiful picture of extravagant worship and being indignant, especially since the money did not come from their own pocket. This is amazing to me. They didn't buy this perfume, spent none of their money for it, and are angry with her.

What looked like excessive devotion to the other followers of Jesus delighted the Lord. "Leave her alone," He commanded. He was so pleased that He made sure this story would be told down through the generations as an example of lavish, costly giving.

I've noticed that women often tend to be more generous than men. In my travels to missionary conventions around the States, I usually host a men's breakfast in addition to the regular meetings we have. While men just need more time, more persuasion to give, women are usually ready to give as soon as they hear of an opportunity. Women have carried the message of Jesus Christ around the world. In some mission fields there are eighteen women to one man. Evidently, according to those statistics, some men are praying, "Here am I, Lord, send my sister." I take my hat off to the women of the world for the price they've willingly paid to take the gospel to the nations.

The most precious gift I ever received came from a poor peasant woman who lived in the mountains of Oaxaca, Mexico. At that time, I was involved in ministry to the Indians of that area. Martha and I had three small children then, so I traveled alone if I knew the trip would be a hardship for the rest of the family.

On that particular trip, I had ridden for seven hours in an ancient Ford truck. Bailing wire held it together, and the back of the truck was full of four tons of merchandise. My driver was a sixteen-year-old boy who maneuvered the sharply winding, narrow roads that led up through a mountain pass. We were driving dangerously close to a precipice that looked down over canyons that were so deep we could not see the bottom. It was raining and those dirt paths were muddy and slippery with no guardrails for protection should we slide too close to the edge.

Just to be on the safe side, I spent the entire seven-hour trip praying and repenting of things I never even thought of doing.

I remembered the time I was in the Navy, serving on the aircraft carrier *Enterprise* in World War II. It was a tough time in my life-- my buddies and I faced death on a regular basis. Surely I hadn't survived kamikaze pilots to let a sixteen-year-old kid kill me on a Mexican mountainside. "O God, keep us safe!" I pleaded.

When we finally arrived at a village called Talea, Oaxaca, I climbed down from the truck and held the first public praise service ever conducted in that pagan village. I was so glad to be alive with my feet on solid ground I didn't care what anyone might think.

To reach my destination, I had to walk for two-and-a-half more hours over muddy trails that wound up and down between the mountains. It was raining and I was carrying Bibles, my sleeping bag, and a suitcase, trying not to fall between the rocks. I would take four steps forward and slip three-and-a-half steps backward. The journey seemed like it would never end.

When I finally arrived at the village where I would be ministering, my feet were in such pain I sat down under a tree and tried to keep from crying. A woman I had never seen before came out of a hut with a pan of cold crystal-clear spring water. Without a word, she knelt at my feet and began to take off my shoes.

Startled by her action, I asked her what she was doing. "I'm going to bathe your feet," was her answer.

"No way," I replied. Mud was caked up to my knees and besides being sore, my feet were odious and filthy.

"Hermano Myers," she spoke in Spanish, "don't rob me, a handmaid of the Lord, the blessing of bathing the feet of a servant of my Lord." Tears were running down her sun-weathered face. I will never forget her humble expression as long as I live. What could I say? She was offering the act as unto the Lord. When I told her she could proceed, she handled my filthy feet like they were costly crystal. I was aware that this wasn't about me. She was doing this as unto the Lord and I began to cry right along with her. In all my years in the ministry, I've never received a more precious gift. That simple, poor woman gave the best she had to the Lord and in that moment, in my eyes, she seemed more important than the President of the Republic of Mexico.

Where did we get the idea that we should give God what we can comfortably afford or don't need anymore? We sometimes pat ourselves on the back for giving used clothes to the poor, or ten extra dollars on top of our tithes. And don't get me wrong. I'm sure that God is pleased with our tithes and offerings, whatever they might be. But there is an added joy in giving God the most precious part of our lives and possessions.

Mary of Bethany poured her costly gift over Jesus' feet, gave it with a heart full of love for her Master. You can't love deeply and be a stingy giver. In the book of Acts when Ananias and Sapphira lied to the Holy Ghost about what they had given, they were judged severely for their sin. Their lying simply covered their selfishness and greed.

It seems the poorest people on the earth understand the concept of lavish giving more than we who live comfortably in the United States with 54 percent of the world's resources at our fingertips.

A woman in the city of Leon, Mexico had no family to care for her, no home, and no income. She was so poor that the pastor added a few boards beside the church and put a tarp over it for shelter and let her stay there. She swept out the church every day and the Christians fed her. Everyone knew that although she had nothing, she loved God with all of her heart. One day she became very ill. When it became apparent that she wasn't going to recover, she called the pastor to her little board bed.

"Pastor, I'm going home to be with Jesus," she said. "I want to leave you everything I've got in this world. Put your hand under this pillow, and whatever you find is yours."

He felt beneath the pillow and found sixty centavos, about a nickel in American money. That's all she had when she died. I can think of no better way to prepare for the other side than to give away all you have before you leave this world.

GIVING WITH THE RIGHT MOTIVE

13

When you give because you can't
help it, you'll receive because
you can't stop it.

*"God's best gifts to us are not things
but opportunities."*

Few people have impacted my life as much as a pastor named "Pop" Morton. I met this wise man of God in Bremerton, Washington, when I was a young man in the Navy. Pop and his wife pastored a small church in that city and opened their home to sailors stationed at the nearby naval base. Despite the fact that he and his wife lived on a meager salary, he often invited my buddies and me over for dinner. Sometimes there were as many as twenty-five of us sitting around their table, enjoying a rare home-cooked meal and some of Pop Morton's spiritual wisdom.

Long after everyone had gone, I sat with this godly man in his little breakfast nook, bombarding him with questions about the ministry. This was a man who loved people and knew God intimately—a powerful combination. God had called me into the ministry and I wanted to learn as much as I could from him because he was so full of love and wisdom. Sometimes, much to the chagrin of his wife, he and I were still talking and discussing scriptures as late as 3:00 in the morning.

Pop Morton died unexpectedly at the age of fifty-one and I was heartbroken. He was my father in the faith. After he died, Mrs. Morton confessed to me that she had begged Pop to spend less time with me. "There are twenty-five other sailors who have more potential than he does," she told him.

"What did he say to that?" I was curious.

"He told me, 'Honey, you take care of the house and I'll take care of Myers. Evidently you don't see what I see in him, but I'm going to pour my life into that boy.'"

He did, and for that I have always been grateful. To this day, some of Pop Morton's words still live inside of me. I remember his exhortation, "Wayne, you'll make many mistakes in the ministry, primarily because you're a novice. With experience you could avoid some of these mistakes, but if you'll keep your motive pure before God, do everything in His name and for His glory, God will empty heaven of its resources for you. If He has to rescue you, He will put angels on half-rations if He needs to. But if you have a wrong motive, Son, you'll tie the hands of God."

After many years of ministry, I still use those words as a spiritual checkup. "Lord, why do I do what I do?" I often pray. "May there not be a tainted motive. May I not work for human recognition, praise, or applause. May everything I do be only for your Kingdom."

Giving is like everything else in our faith walk. It must be done out of a pure heart with right motives. *"Keep and guard your heart with all vigilance and above all that you guard, for out of it flow the springs of life,"* (Proverbs 4:23 AMPLIFIED)

Some people are ignorant of the fact that it is possible to give with wrong motives and grieve the heart of God.

When Ananias and his wife Sapphira sold a piece of property, they brought part of the proceeds to Peter as an offering. According to their recorded story in Acts 5, they deceived the brethren as to the amount they had received as profit from the sale. Their sin was not that they had not given enough money, but that they both attempted to deceive the Holy Spirit.

"…and even after it was sold, was not the money at your disposal and under your control?" Peter asked. They could have done anything they wanted to with their money, but after they had attempted to use their offering to deceive and manipulate, they, along with their money, were cursed. Husband and wife died instantly.

There is danger in commercializing our giving for the sake of personal gain. You can't commercialize with God. You can't buy the blessings of God. Ananias and Sapphira are both a graphic lesson to remind us not to try to cheat God and call it economy.

The message of prosperity has been abused, and poorly taught. I believe that God prospers us for the purpose of blessing someone else—not just for our own gain. When I teach on the subject of giving, I always tell people not to grab for prosperity unless they are sure they can handle it. If your values regarding money have not been changed, if you're still living in the shallow water of deception, the very blessing God wants to give you will become a snare. The only lasting good that a pile of money can do is in its distribution.

> *Money makes a beautiful servant, but a terrible master. Either you control it or it controls you.*

Ministries and churches have been destroyed because of a wrong understanding of money. Someone said it very well: *"When a man prospers, God either gains a partner or Satan gains a fool."*

Paul wrote to Timothy, *"For the love of money is a root of all kinds of evil. Some people, eager for money, have wandered from the faith and pierced themselves with many griefs"* (I Timothy 6:10 NIV).

Money makes a beautiful servant, but a terrible master. Either you control it or it controls you. Either you are a master of the things God puts in your hands or those very things will sell you short. A wrong motive toward money will rob you of every eternal value.

In Los Cocos, Mexico, a Christian woman approached her pastor with great excitement. "Pastor, I just sold my mango crop for 25,000 pesos ($2,000)." She was incredulous with how God had blessed her. "Why, they didn't even ask me to harvest the fruit off the trees. Their offer includes picking the fruit themselves!"

Although she was a member of the church, she did not tithe on her profitable sale. Instead, she brought the pastor one peso, the equivalent of eight cents—the price of a Pepsi Cola©. She hid the rest of the 25,000 pesos in a wooden box.

Two weeks later, her house caught on fire and burned to the ground. She lost everything, including the wooden box full of pesos. On top of that catastrophe, the Papaloapan River near her home began to flood and swept many of her cattle downstream.

God didn't punish this woman. But if we violate divine principles, we cancel out divine promises. I believe her disobedience broke down God's wall of protection. It is not what we possess, but what possesses us that determines our value before God and man. In fact, I believe that the true value of a person is what he or she would be worth if they lost everything.

The right motive in giving is love. I urge people around the world to give—not from the top of your purse, but from the bottom of your heart. When we give from the bottom of our heart, we are giving in the same spirit that Jesus gave when He said, *"No man takes my life, I give it"* (John 10:18). We must walk in the footsteps of Jesus. He didn't come to get, He came to give, even His own life. He said, "As my Father has sent me, even so send I you." God sends us out to bless others by our lives, our testimony, our witness, our talents, and our possessions.

How God loves you! Yes, He wants you in a place of blessing, with every bill paid and prospering financially. But He also wants to see your heart pure from every trace of greed, resentment, hatred, and bitterness. Don't seek prosperity unless you've got enough of God in your life to wisely distribute the abundance.

REFUSING TO GIVE TO GET

I strongly believe in the natural and spiritual law of sowing and reaping. If you sow into the kingdom of God, you will be blessed, but don't give to get. Give with right motives—because you can't help it, because you love Him. Give because you love His kingdom. Give because things don't bind you. Always take control over things, don't let things control you.

When we give because we can't help it, we receive because we can't stop it. *"Whatever you do in word or deed, do all in the name of Jesus, giving glory to the Father through Him"* (Colossians 3:17). It doesn't matter if people recognize it or not. God sees it. Give out of a heart full of love and gratitude for his glory.

Man says to God, "Give me a lot
and I'll give you something."
God says to man, "Give me a lot of
your little and I'll give you more."

*"He who keeps close to God will not
be cheap with God."*

I have had to eat a lot of crow in my day. And I can tell you that no matter how you season it, it's not very tasty—nor is it easy to say grace over. But for most of us, the lessons we learn the hard way are the ones we never forget.

Once I had been living in the mountains of Mexico, ministering to the Indians. In order to reach their village, I had to fly in an old B17 and land on a makeshift runway so primitive that we had to buzz the strip to get the slow, fat cows off of it before we could land.

On this particular trip, I had been in those mountains for two weeks and had hardly slept during that time. Without the benefit of DDT, the bedbug population in the village had mushroomed. I've always said that one bedbug in anyone's bed is a majority, but a thousand bedbugs is a prelude to hell. I could hardly wait to get back to the city for a good night's sleep. I was irritable and tired and to make matters worse, I had five pesos (equivalent to one American dollar) and seven one-dollar bills to my name.

When I arrived at the airport in Mexico City, I realized I'd need to hire a taxi, so I checked the fare ahead of time to make sure I had enough money to get home.

"It's five pesos if you go by yourself," someone told me. "But if you share the cab with someone else it's only three." Obviously, I was going to share a taxi. When I arrived home, I gave my five pesos to the driver and waited for my change, but he had no intention of giving me what was rightfully mine.

"Sir, the fare is three pesos because you have another client. I believe you owe me two pesos." It was obvious that he would not budge and I was angry.

"Sir, the Bible talks about you," I said. "It calls you a thief. It also speaks of your eternal destiny of burning in hell."

Well, I won. He gave me the two pesos and I walked into my house proud of the fact that he had not been able to cheat me. The victory was short lived. When I couldn't find the rest of the money, I realized I must have dropped the seven dollar bills on the seat of the taxi. I had no sooner set my bag down when I heard a voice coming up from somewhere in the vicinity of my spirit,

"That was quite a show you put on out there on the street. You know what you did, son, don't you? You sent that poor man to hell and you didn't even give him a chance to go to heaven."

"Yes, Lord, I know, but I don't like thieves. Every time I get in a taxi, they try to rob me." I figured I had made a good defense of my position. I was wrong. God was still speaking to me:

"So the servant is above His Master? I died between two thieves.".

The sad ending to this story is that I had argued over thirty-five cents and ruined my testimony, and so God saw to it that I had left my last seven dollars on the seat as an *involuntary tip.*

It was a hard lesson at the time and one I have never forgotten. It is always more difficult to operate in a generous spirit when we are in need ourselves. Why on earth would God require anyone to give when they need money themselves? Isn't He a giver with unlimited resources? Shouldn't someone else do the giving when we find ourselves in tough financial situations?

I mentioned before the woman in 1 Kings 17 who was so poor she had just enough meal and oil to make one last cake before she starved to death. Imagine the prophet of God having the audacity to ask for her last cake. He had been eating by the brook for the last two-and-a-half years—bread and meat in the morning and bread and meat in the evening. How *dare* he ask a widow woman with a starving son to feed.

Through His prophet's request for that meal, God shows us the powerful principle that turned her poverty into a successful solution for her dire circumstances. They not only ate one more meal from that empty barrel, but the three of them ate for one whole year. This same principle will work every time for you and me. It is simply this: don't wait to give until you can afford it. Give out of your need and watch God honor your gift every time with His over-abundant supply.

I remember one time when I was working as an unmarried missionary. I hadn't seen an offering in so long that I'd forgotten whose face was on the dollar bill. My sister, who occasionally sent me money, sent me a ten-dollar bill. For me, it was like coming into an inheritance. I was so happy to get that offering and thought, *"O my, I'm going to get to eat a little better now."*

As clear as a bell I heard God say, "Son, I want you to send that ten dollar bill to a missionary in southern Mexico."

I said, "God, you must be kidding. You can't be serious."

I had to pray all night to let go of that ten dollars. The next morning I was actually glad to get rid of it so I could get some rest. When the missionary received it, he wrote, "Brother Myers, I have two small children and we were out of milk and had no money when we got your offering." Suddenly, I was very glad I had obeyed God.

The law of sowing and reaping has been overused often by those who are building their own kingdom on earth. Some use this biblical principle to manipulate people to give to their ministries. But that doesn't change the power of this truth that will work in the natural as well as the spiritual. Genesis 8:22 says that as long as the world exists, there will be seed time and harvest.

I grew up on a farm and watched my Dad as he sowed crops. I learned principles from watching him work with seeds and dirt that impact me to this day. First, the seed of harvest was always the seed of sowing. He never sowed beans and reaped sweet potatoes. Second, he always reaped in proportion to how much he sowed.

One day while sowing beans he said, "Son, I'm tired. I want you to finish this field. When you've finished planting these two sacks of beans you can go to the house." It was the wrong information to give a boy who wanted to get out of the hot sun and the back-breaking job of planting seeds into the ground. I began to sow beans faster than they had ever been sown before, dropping them on top of each other in my effort to get back to the house.

We had never harvested a bean crop like the one we had that year. It wasn't evenly distributed over the field, but it was bountiful because that's how I sowed it.

Sowing our crop when we have little seed requires faith in the ability of God to come through for us. It takes faith to release something you think you can't live without. For instance, it takes faith to pray in a car when you haven't got one, and even more faith to give it away after you have prayed it in.

I was in Lancaster, Pennsylvania, speaking in a Mennonite church, teaching the people how to give. After the sermon, we began to raise money for missionaries in many different countries. One of the brothers there had just recently been saved and was full of faith and enthusiasm. Each time we extended an opportunity to give to one of their missionaries, he responded by raising his hand and stating the amount he would give. By the end of the evening he had pledged a significant amount of money. After the service I discovered that this brother didn't even have a job.

Now his was a stretch of faith if I ever heard one. I knew that either this man was not fully aware of what he was doing, or he was on his way to becoming a millionaire. Anyone who has a heart to please God and who trusts God to not only meet his needs, but to bless others through him, will prosper.

When I returned to that church four years later, this same man came up and greeted me. "Do you remember me?" he asked. "I'm the man who you said either had a loose screw in his coconut or would be a millionaire. Well, the last part of your prophecy came true. In the last four years, I have made four million dollars."

> *Anyone who has a heart to please God and who trusts God to not only meet his needs but to bless others through him, will prosper.*

I'm not saying that everyone who gives generously will become a millionaire. But the Bible says, *"a generous man will himself be blessed"* (Proverbs 22:9). The same basic principle in Galatians 6:7 says, *"Whatever a man sows, that's what he will reap."* In Proverbs 11:25 we read, *"A liberal soul shall be made fat and he that blesses others will be blessed himself."*

Jorge Galvan was a young student whom Martha and I sponsored in Bible school. He later pioneered a church in a poor area of Mexico where the gospel needed to be preached. One new church member, a father of five children, invited Jorge to eat with him every day.

One day, Jorge told him, "Listen, I can't eat with you every day like this. You have a wife and five children to feed and I know that you don't make more than five pesos a day."

"Pastor, please don't punish my children," the man pleaded.

Astonished, Jorge asked, "What do you mean, 'don't punish your children?'"

"When you eat with us we have tortillas left over," was the father's reply, "but when you don't eat with us, we don't have enough."

Giving pleases God because it requires faith in His unquestionable character. *"Look at the birds of the air,"* He tells us in Matthew 6. God knows them all and feeds them every day without fail. The richest man in the world couldn't feed all of the birds on earth for one day, and yet God does it, day after day. And He is not any poorer for it. If He cares for the birds in this way, how much more does He delight in taking care of His people?

When we step out in faith by giving what we have, He increases our storehouse to give more. You know you are becoming more like God, the great Giver, when you live a life of giving—even in the face of your own need. I am a firm believer in what my friend, the late Costa Deir once said, *"The more we love and give, the more like Jesus we live."*

Man has as much of God as he is
willing to give away.

*"You can give without loving, but
you can't love without giving."*

For a young man looking for action, the USS Enterprise, the most decorated ship in Naval history, was the place to be. She had sunk more enemy ships and shot down more enemy planes than any other carrier in the Pacific. She was credited for changing the course of the Second World War.

As a young seaman, this famous war vessel was my home for nineteen months, and my ticket to adventure. I found myself on my way to the Marshall Islands, green and seasick, but willing to defend my country.

I had come a long way from my roots in Morton, Mississippi. Instead of harvesting corn, beans, and cotton on my parents' 160-acre farm, I was in the middle of the Pacific, fighting a dangerous war. My buddies and I lived with the constant threat of bombers overhead and torpedoes underneath. Our lives were literally perched between heaven and hell in a world where death could happen at any time.

It was time for spiritual inventory. When a friend invited me to join a prayer meeting one night on the flight deck, I accepted. I had received Jesus Christ as my Savior in the little Baptist Church where Mother and Dad were members, and I was baptized with my cousin in a nearby creek. But now, away from all that was secure and normal, I realized I needed inner strength to face the fear and danger that were part of my daily schedule.

I walked on the deck one night and found a group of men in the moonlight in a circle, praying. These tough Navy seamen were taking turns talking to God as if He were very near. I sat there in amazement. I had never been around a group of people so intimate with Jesus Christ. These guys were a breed apart.

One of the sailors' prayers gave me the fright of my life. He was weeping and praying the most radical prayer I had ever heard,

"Lord, if any man has to die in this battle, let it be one of us because we know You."

When he prayed, "One of us," I thought, *he is including me and I'm just a visitor.* I almost stopped him and said, "Speak for yourself, Mac. I don't want to die for anybody. I want to go home."

I had never seen that kind of love for Jesus, and it left a deep impression on my life. The idea of giving my life away was not only uncomfortable, it was unthinkable.

THE ULTIMATE GIFT

Since then, I have learned that you cannot separate being a Christian from laying down your life. After all, it was Jesus who taught us this principle by His example: *"The Son of Man did not come to be served, but to serve, and to give His life"* (Matthew 20:28 NIV).

When we think of giving, we oftentimes think of material things—our possessions or our money. But that's a small area of serving and giving in a Christian's life. Writing a check is sometimes far easier than giving God our time and energy.

God has called us to express our love with whatever He puts into our hands—whether it's our time, talents, or resources. Growing in spiritual maturity precludes our obedience in all of these areas.

LIVING TO SERVE

The word *service* (or *serve*) is found over 1,400 times in the Bible. It is at the heart of the gospel. But we Christians often look for position, rather than for opportunities. For most of us, it is harder to pick up a towel or broom. Remember James and John, the two disciples who put in their application for the two highest positions in the kingdom. They asked their mother to intercede for Jesus to seat them next to Him on His throne. Like mothers everywhere, she wanted her boys taken care of and approached Jesus with her bold request:

"Grant that one of these two sons of mine may sit at your right and the other at your left in your kingdom" (Matthew 20:21 NIV). After telling her (and her sons) that the Father would give those positions to whom they had been prepared, Jesus took the opportunity to teach all of His disciples about greatness. *"...but whosoever will be great among you, let him be your servant"* (Matthew 20:26).

In the world, greatness is defined in one way; in God's Kingdom, another way.

Someone said, "He who gets wrapped up in himself makes a very small package." You may have enough sermon tapes to evangelize Texas, but unless you are willing to share your life, your message isn't going to go far. Ultimately, it doesn't matter how beautifully you sing or how well you pray in church, but what you do with your life. The world doesn't care how much you know until it knows how much you care. We express that with our deeds—not just with our words.

We have a mission on earth, given by God, and it is to serve. We must walk in the footsteps of Jesus—He didn't come to get, He came to give. He said, *"As my Father has sent me, even so send I you"* (John 20:21).

We are being sent out to bless a world by our lives, our testimony, our witness, our talents, and our possessions. Every day we rub shoulders with people that we can impact for eternity, by serving them.

SIMPLE SERVING

We convert the temporal into the eternal by making it a practice to share our life and resources every day. *"Who can I bless today, Lord?"* is a powerful prayer that God is delighted to answer. They are all around us—the broken, the poor, the wounded. And unless we are willing to share with them, we'll live in a very small world. If you are determined to play it safe, you'll play a very small game.

Like giving God monetary gifts, it is folly to wait until what you have to offer seems important. A Christian hug isn't going to cost you anything and many times it makes the difference in someone's day. A simple word of encouragement at the right moment can make the difference in someone's life—or even their destiny. All of us can take time to pray with a friend who is discouraged...or give a generous gift to a poor waitress... or slip a five-dollar bill into someone's hand. It is called *thinking eternal.* We learn to buy up every opportunity to bless and serve.

I don't know how many thousands of meals my wife has prepared through our years of ministry. Neighbors, local ministers, uneducated and poor friends, and government officials have sat around our table. After an evening of Martha's mouth-watering cooking and relaxed conversation, many gave their hearts to the Lord. Others received the baptism of the Holy Spirit or were encouraged to keep walking through dark times and not give up. I couldn't possibly count the hundreds of lives that

> *We convert the temporal into the eternal by making it a practice to share our life and resources every day.*

have been changed through this simple act of serving.

Aurelio and Ivonne Arrache, a young couple whose marriage was in trouble, were two of those people we invited to dinner one evening. Aurelio was an efficiency expert at a bank and yet, because he was an alcoholic, he couldn't report to work on time. Ivonne was a recently converted Christian and much to the chagrin of her unbelieving husband, had invited us to hold meetings in their home.

After dinner, it seemed natural to ask him if he was ready to give his heart to the Lord. He was and he did. When we explained about the baptism of the Holy Spirit and suggested he might as well go ahead and receive this experience as well, Aurelio was ready. He had been reading his wife's books on the Holy Spirit in order to refute her testimony, but he told us later, that the love and peace in our home had disarmed him. He left our living room a changed man, saved and filled with the Holy Spirit.

Ivonne told us that the next morning she woke up at 5:00 A.M, startled that Aurelio was not in bed. She found him kneeling at their bedside, praying fervently. It was the first sign that their marriage and home would never be the same.

Aurelio later explained that when he was down on his knees, he asked God questions that were troubling him. *Now that he was a Christian, could he have a happy home? And what about his wife and their marriage problems? Was it O.K. to drink alcoholic beverages now? And the strange language that had come out of his mouth in prayer... what was that?*

After prayer, he opened his Bible and read: *"Husbands love your wives just as Christ loved the church and gave himself up for her..."* (Ephesians 5:25 NIV). In the same chapter he read, *"Do not get drunk with wine, but be filled with the Holy Spirit"* (Ephesians 5:18).

He turned to 2 Corinthians and found that tongues are a language given by God to speak directly to God and not man. Although his faith was less than one day old, he had grown through that one personal encounter with God.

S P I R I T S   A N D   R A T T L E S N A K E S

Martha and I watched Aurelio grow in his new faith. All seemed to be going well until he made a trip to Bogotá, Columbia, to teach a group of bankers.

I was deeply troubled about the trip and didn't know why. I felt a strong urge to pray for Aurelio. When he returned, I drove to his home and asked him what was wrong.

"Nothing," he replied.

"Yes, there is." I persevered. "I have a burden for you. Tell me what happened in Bogotá."

"Well, before I realized what was happening, the bankers offered me cocktails, and I began to drink again.

"I heard the guilt and self-condemnation in his voice and knew he was struggling with the battle with alcohol again. I looked over and saw the well-stocked bar in Aurelio's house. Even though he had made a commitment to not drink anymore, he had hundreds of dollars worth of expensive bottles of alcohol. It was somewhat of a status symbol and he reasoned that it was too expensive to throw out.

I asked Aurelio a question, "Aurelio, if you had a rattlesnake in your house, what would the wiser testimony be—to say that you tip-toed around that snake for six months and hadn't been bitten—or that you had found the deadly reptile in your house and killed it?"

Aurelio knew where I was headed with that illustration. "It

would be wiser to kill it," he replied.

"I'll buy all of that liquor in your bar and we'll pour it down the toilet together," I challenged him.

"Brother Myers, that's a lot of money. I can't accept that kind of gift from you because I'm behind on my tithes," he answered. "I already owe God."

I convinced him to accept my offer and we began opening bottles and pouring the "spirits" down the toilet together. I'd never drank in my life and had no idea how much money we were flushing away that day. Aurelio has not touched a drink since.

Not long after that, Ivonne and Aurelio moved close to the U.S. border and began to hold evangelistic meetings. They hosted teas and dinners, inviting people who would never normally go to church to hear the gospel. In the past twenty-three years, that couple has won over 40,000 souls to Christ. Aurelio bought a defunct Karate club for a quarter of a million dollars and established a 1,500 member church. It has been a tremendous ministry and many churches have been born out of that one church. Last December, I preached at their church's twenty-third anniversary service.

SERVE UNSELFISHLY

We don't always see the immediate results of the time, prayers, and love we pour into another individual. However, the principle is the same whether we are giving away our money, or time, or gifts, or abilities. We are laying up treasure on the other side.

Cooking a meal, giving someone your time, being willing to pray when it's not convenient...these are gifts that bear eternal results. Being willing to be used by God to serve someone else always has a cost. When I teach young, eager Bible students who want to go into the ministry, I remind them that the greatest leaders of the world are those who never look for position. Great leaders are great servants.

There's never been a statue of eternal value made to honor a man who lived selfishly. But there are many monuments to men who left big footprints in the sands of church history through their lives of servanthood.

David Livingstone's life's theme was, "Anywhere, Lord, as long as it's forward." I like that. I also like George Whitfield's testimony. He said, "I'm willing to go to jail and death with you, but I'm not willing to go to heaven without you." That's the kind of love that's taking the gospel around the world.

When we put God first, we will automatically serve others. In fact, we only put Him first as we serve others. Jesus said, *"As much as ye did it to the least of these—the hungry, the naked, the lame, the blind, the needy—you did it unto Me."* Our debt to God is payable to man. God is looking for those who will walk in the arena of service.

SILENT SERVING

True servants are willing to work, quietly and unseen, behind the scenes. They don't clamor for the spotlight. They fulfill their assignments with all their heart, never concerning themselves with a need to be first. These are the ones Jesus spoke of when He said, *"The first shall be last and the last shall be first"* (Mark 9:35).

One of God's greatest servants that I was privileged to know for forty-nine years was Elizabeth Clark, a woman from Fairfield, Texas. She served Martha and me faithfully all those years by praying for us. Many times when we were in danger from accidents, fanatical mobs' ambushes, or our children's illnesses, the Holy Spirit would alert her to pray. I have no doubt in my mind that when Martha and I stand before the Lord on that day, Elizabeth Clark will be standing with us, to receive an equal share in any eternal treasures that we have laid up on the other side.

GOD'S MULTIPLICATION TABLE

When we serve God by giving him our money, He multiplies it, enlarges His kingdom through it, and gives more back to us. In the same way, when we serve God by laying down our lives for our brothers, He multiplies the effort we've made and increases the fruitfulness of our lives. Elizabeth Clark's prayers helped to change the nation of Mexico.

My wife, Martha, cooked delicious dinners and fed the spiritually hungry, multiplying the number of Christians whose lives were changed forever. The Lord used the same miraculous principle in our case as He did when He fed the 5,000 with a boy's small lunch. When we give what we have, God will always use it to bless more people than we could ever imagine. Someone has said, "Man lives in the area of addition. Satan lives in the area of subtraction. But God's specialty is in multiplication."

The key to an overflowing, exuberant life of joy and significance is to live as Jesus lived on earth—a Servant who gave His all.

SACRIFICIAL GIVING

16

You can no more empty your
pocket through giving than you
can empty your heart
through loving.

*"A man does not own his wealth,
he owes it."*

Many years ago while in Central Mexico, I learned about sacrificial giving. The Mexican brothers there were dear friends who had remained faithful to the Lord through many tribulations. In fact, many Christian martyrs had given the ultimate sacrifice of their lives. When one of the pastors asked if I would help him build the roof on a new church in that area, I gladly accepted.

After ministering to the church members on the joy of giving, I had promised that Martha and I would give the first $400 toward the completion of the new building. Dear Martha is used to my giving faith promises in her name as well as in mine. In fact, she was a giver before we were married. In our fifty years of ministry together, she has never complained about the offerings that come out of our budget. She always helps me pray the money in and never panics when we don't see where the finances will come from to pay our commitment.

Actually, $400 didn't seem like a large sum to me, as we had often promised much larger amounts of money. God had always supplied the resources. I knew if I was going to teach the members of this large church to give, I would have to be an example to let them see I believed in what I was teaching.

After several weeks passed and I still didn't have the money to pay my faith promise, I became concerned. No matter how hard I prayed, it seemed that God was taking a vacation and had a closed office with no one answering the phone.

"Lord, we've always kept our word," I prayed. Nothing has been so important to me as keeping my word. My dad taught me that my word was my bond. Honesty and integrity are the foundation of any ministry. I knew that whatever the cost, I had to honor what I had promised.

Eight weeks passed. I became desperate. I searched my heart for sin and asked God to reveal any blockages that would hinder my prayers. Still no answer.

I knew that I could not let those dear people down. They were expecting a roof on their building and I was fully expecting to do my part to see that they had the money to buy one.

I would have sold my car, but it had a U.S. license. The only things of value that Martha and I possessed were two used manual typewriters, my Bulova watch, and Martha's refrigerator.

"Lord, would you please speak to Martha about selling her refrigerator?" I needed help on this one. Poor Martha didn't even have a living room set. I could hardly ask her to give up her refrigerator. I waited for three days for God to speak to her, praying the whole time. She seemed to be hard of hearing, but on the third day she came to me.

"Honey, we can sell the refrigerator and pay our commitment," she said.

"You bet we can!" I almost jumped for joy. Now I could sell the watch, the two typewriters, and our refrigerator. I finally had the money for our offering.

When I returned to the church to pay our commitment, I spoke on giving again, this time a message I titled, "Can God prepare a table in the wilderness?" But I was still perplexed. Why hadn't God come through for us? At the end of the sermon, the congregation gave enough to complete the building fund for the new church. In spite of the fact that I had not asked them to give watches, the offering bag was full of them. We gathered up seventeen wristwatches and $800 in cash that night. The roof was paid for.

The Greater Blessing

Still, I wasn't through talking with God. I wasn't angry, just deeply perplexed. I knew this could lead to discouragement, and so I stayed in an attitude of prayer until the matter was solved. "Lord, I don't understand. Why didn't you send the money?"

"Son, do you remember what you preached the night you promised the $400?" God was speaking to my heart and I was listening.

"Yes, I remember." I had preached on Nehemiah, "Arise and let us build, for the Lord shall help us."

He said, "That's right, but you made a statement in the message. You told those people that God always blesses a giver, but that there's a special blessing in sacrificial giving. I wanted to see if you would practice what you preach."

"Thank you, Lord. I'll watch my mouth from now on!"

Two months later, Martha had a better refrigerator, the new two-door model with a freezer unit up above. I had a Longine watch and two good typewriters.

The fact that our few possessions had been replaced with better ones weren't the most valuable gifts we received from that experience. Giving sacrificially had stretched us both, propelling us to a new dimension in our giving. In the process, we had increased our capacity for joy and found a great inner freedom. I discovered that when we release something we thought we couldn't live without, we experience release in the process. Our spirits are lighter, our countenance brighter, when we conquer our dependence on possessions for security.

Sacrificial giving cleanses our motives. When we give sacrificially, we don't give to get. We give because we love Him. Because we love

His kingdom. When we give sacrificially, we are proving that possessions don't have a hold on us.

> *When we give sacrificially, we are proving that possessions don't have a hold on us.*

WHEN GIVING IS A SACRIFICE

King David knew the power of bending low in humility and submission and making a sacrifice to God. When he numbered the children of Israel against the counsel of God, he transgressed God's authority and grieved Him. David asked Ornan, the owner of the threshing floor, where God had instructed him to offer a sacrifice, to let him buy his property so that he could worship God with his gift. Ornan, who wanted to honor God and King David, offered to give not only the threshing floor, but the oxen for the offering, the wood to burn it, and the wheat for the meat offering as well.

"It's all yours," he told David. "No strings attached."

David refused: *"Nay, but I will verily buy it for the full price; for I will not take that which is thine for the Lord, nor offer burnt offerings without cost"* (1 Chronicles 21:24 KJV).

David was not satisfied in giving God a gift that he had received from someone else. Such an offering could hardly be described as a sacrifice. He knew that to be of value to God, his offering must represent a giving up of something of value to himself.

According to Webster, one of the meanings of sacrifice is "to give one's life." The concept scares most of us because it means that some kind of death is involved. Most of us would rather avoid anything that affects our lifestyle or personal comfort.

Blessed is the man who places his heart alongside his gift on the altar of sacrifice. We are not only offering our money to God when we give sacrificially, we worship Him with the attitude that says, "You, O God, are worth everything I have, everything I own." Sacrificial giving, like audible praise, is a sweet-smelling aroma, confirming His Lordship over our possessions and us.

A sacrificial gift means more in God's eyes than a large gift that costs us nothing. Jesus used the story of the poor widow who offered her last copper coins to teach us this principle: "I tell you the truth," He said, "this poor widow has put in more than all the others. All these people gave their gifts out of their wealth, but she out of her poverty put in all she had to live on."

Those two small coins thrilled Jesus more than the large sums of money put in the offering that day, because this woman gave her food money, her rent money—all that she had—because of her love for the Lord. He is still talking about it today, making sure we remember her example, by recording it for all time in His Word. That's the power of a sacrificial gift given with a pure heart motive.

You can't separate the way you handle the temporal from the way you handle the eternal. They are one package. To know your depth in God, loan me your checkbook and I'll tell you. It's your spiritual dipstick, just as reliable as the one used to gauge the level of oil in your car. Jesus' whole life was one of sacrifice. He didn't just tell us that He loved us. He proved it by giving everything He had for our salvation. And everything He gave cost Him: coming to earth, being separated from the Father, suffering the rejection of men, and finally the ultimate sacrifice, His life. The moment we experienced salvation, we received the sacrificial gift that He gave.

Receiving and giving sacrificially are two different experiences, but both need to flow in and out of our life in proportion to the grace we have received.

RECEIVING SACRIFICIAL GIFTS

Receiving sacrificial gifts can sometimes be as hard as giving sacrificially. I have been in remote villages where Indian women walked long distances to bring me one egg. That was all they had. Other times, out of courtesy to my host, I've had to eat the last chicken in the yard of a family, their small children watching me. These kinds of gifts broke my heart and humbled my soul, but I know the principle of giving will work in their lives just as it has in mine. We do no favor when we teach the poor that God does not expect them to give. On the contrary, it is a grave injustice because we rob them of the opportunity to move into a dimension that guarantees their daily bread.

UNLIMITED 17 POTENTIAL

A life spent in the service of God
and in communion with Him is
the happiest life that anyone can
live in this world.

*"The more we love and give,
the more like God we live."*

No one who knew me as a child growing up in Mississippi would have chosen me as a candidate for an extraordinary lifestyle. If you had told me that I would someday travel the world and watch people's lives change and see church buildings erected to the glory of God, I would not have believed you. In fact, no one else would have either.

When I was five years old, I fell on a corner of a doorstep, injured my lower abdomen, and developed severe peritonitis. For the next ten years of my life, I underwent multiple operations and lived with severe pain. The injury stole my childhood and crippled my parent's finances. They finally mortgaged our Mississippi farm in a desperate effort to pay the hospital bills. It was not a great start to life.

After I encountered Christ in a life-changing way, I begged God to use me any way He wanted. I was an unlikely candidate—poor health, no great education, no money, and no influential people to back me. I imagined the conversation in heaven over my prayer. God the Father could have said to His Son, "Son, who is the greatest challenge that we have on the drawing board today?"

"Well, Father, there's Myers down there bugging us," I could imagine Jesus replying. Evidently, the Father must have said, "Let's risk it." At least that's the only way I can figure out why God would choose me to partner with Him.

The only thing I had going for me as a young man who longed to be in ministry was that I loved to pray. It turned out to be the one thing I needed most. *On my knees I learned everything I would need for the next fifty-six years of ministry: how to hear the voice of God and how to pour out my worship at His feet.* The result was an increasing faith in His ability to do the impossible in my life.

One of the first assignments God gave me in the ministry was to return to the town of a few thousand people where I had grown up and preach on the streets. When I told the Lord I would go, I also told him what I lacked in order to do the job well. I had no preaching experience, no P.A. system, and no musical instrument to use to draw a crowd. (Not that I could have played one if I did.)

It was a tough first assignment. "How am I going to preach to these people?" I asked God in prayer.

"Go to the printer and print up 500 cards and pass them out all over town." I knew the idea was from God. I followed His instructions and handed out my cards. When the meeting time came, the streets were blocked with people in every direction to see the sickly child who grew up and joined the Navy. Word was out that I had been under quite a bit of stress in the war and had become religious. I think most of them came out to confirm my insanity.

It didn't matter to me why they came, just that they did. I was young and inexperienced, but I also had a passionate love for God. I preached my heart out and nineteen people were bold enough to kneel on a public street and give their hearts to God. A church started with those nineteen converts, and it continues to this day. I recently met with one of the original members, who was saved in that church, and he said, "You know, Wayne, there are more than a dozen preachers who came out of that little church."

It's a good thing for most of us, that according to 1 Corinthians, God doesn't choose us based on our physical strength, intelligence, or popularity. Paul said that He has purposely chosen the weak and despised so that none could brag about what we've done.

Most of us don't fall into God's great plan for our life in one giant leap. We learn how to give what is in our hand, no matter how small our gift is, and watch God multiply it. We can't begin to know the potential of our prayers, or our gifts, or our talents when we give them in the name of the Lord and serve Him with all our heart.

I asked a pastor friend how he came to know the Lord.

"A Methodist Christian gave me a New Testament," he told me. "I took it home and shared it with my family. Our family of eight was saved. I loaned it to my neighbor and his family of nine was saved."

Two churches and three preachers were birthed out of that ten-cent Bible. That's the power of giving. You never know what God will do through your life or mine if we move into this realm of faith that giving requires.

If you want to reach your full potential as a giver, here are some suggestions:

1. Stay away from negative people.
2. Expect a return on your giving.
3. Practice doing the impossible.

STAY AWAY FROM NEGATIVE PEOPLE

Did I tell you about the woman who married a pessimist? She could not please that man no matter how hard she tried. He criticized her soup, he criticized her coffee, he even criticized the way she wore her hair. Finally, in desperation, she got up early one morning to pray for God's help.

"Oh God, help me please my husband through breakfast. I haven't got faith for all day, so just help me make him happy through breakfast." She went in with the best smile she had and said, "Honey, what do you want for breakfast?"

"One egg scrambled and one egg fried," he mumbled.

This dutiful wife carefully fried one egg, making sure the yolk didn't break in the process. She then scrambled the second egg and took both out to her husband. So far so good. Perhaps they would have a happy breakfast after all.

It was not to be. A few minutes later, she heard her husband calling her. "Come here, woman. Can't you do anything right? You scrambled the wrong egg."

I think God would have said, "Hit him for me." You can't help pessimistic Christians, so I avoid them. They will assault your faith, and if you let them, they will warn you of all the reasons you should not step out in faith.

EXPECT A RETURN ON YOUR GIVING

People who live beyond the possible live expectantly. You have never met a farmer who planted seeds for his crop just because he enjoyed the process. Everything in our hand is a seed to be given away. Everything in God's hand is a harvest. When we plant our seed, He gives His harvest just as surely as night follows day.

Don't expect a harvest until you release your seed. You can't reap before you sow. As soon as the seed leaves your hand, the harvest begins. If you sow enough seed, the harvest will feed you.

PRACTICE DOING THE IMPOSSIBLE

F.G. Myer said that we'll never know the extent of God's resources until we dare to do the impossible. Everyone who has lived up to their full potential as movers and shakers in God's Kingdom has had to step out into the unknown.

Those who live beyond the possible live a lifestyle distinct from the norm. You will never hear them subscribing to the philosophy of "live and let live." On the contrary, God's people are a breed apart. They're made from a different mold than the world. Imagine David, a lad, taking on a giant, or Abraham moving out to a new country without knowing where it was.

> *Unless you are giving more to God's kingdom today than you did last week, you will eventually stagnate.*

I like to rub shoulders with people who think big, stand tall, live holy, defy the devil, and take the prey from his grip. They dare to build a road through uncharted terrain to the glory of God. They travel from victory to victory, from one challenge to another. Their lives are an inspiration to some and a rebuke to others. When we live this kind of life, we honor the Lord who said in Jeremiah 32:27, *"Behold, I am the Lord, the God of all flesh. Is anything too hard for Me?"*

It is impossible to grow without giving. If you want to fulfill your full potential, then give yourself away. Unless you are giving more to God's kingdom today than you did last week, you will eventually stagnate.

A task with a vision is the hope
of the future.

*"Don't cheat the Lord and
call it economy."*

We live in a day of tremendous pressure. Newspapers herald daily tales of terror and strike fear in households across the nation. Corporations are filing bankruptcy, leaving thousands without jobs, while investors check the pulse of the stock market daily, fearing financial doom.

Satan is doing his best to wear down the saints. If the enemy of our soul can cause us to live under stress, worry, and fear, then he has accomplished his primary goal. Fretting over what we can't keep, in exchange for what we can't lose, will defeat us.

Never be afraid to trust your unknown financial future to a known God. Paul, writing to the Corinthian church in 2 Corinthians 2:14 says, *"Thanks be unto God who always causes us to triumph in Christ Jesus."*

> *Never be afraid to trust your unknown financial future to a known God.*

God's bookkeeping is excellent and His memory has no blanks. He knows where you are, He knows your need, and He is concerned about the things that concern you. He wants to show you His greatness.

My life is proof of God's faithfulness. On the fifth of March, I will have spent fifty-six years in the beautiful land of Mexico among some of the most precious people God ever created. After fifty-six years of trusting Him to supply every need, I have no cause to worry about finances. I am confident that no matter the circumstances around me, God always has ample provision.

Through the years, I've learned that there are certain things that you must do if you intend to excel in the area of finances.

INSPECT YOUR ATTITUDE

Your attitude determines your altitude. Don't adopt the world's mindset regarding money. Instead, base your faith on the Word of God and you will see what God will do for you.

Our attitude is a result of what we put in our mind, so it is important that we keep our minds renewed in the Word of God. Paul offers prudent counsel for the times we live in: *"Finally, brethren, whatsoever things are true, whatsoever things are honest, whatsoever things are just, whatsoever things are pure, whatsoever things are lovely, whatsoever things are of good report, if there be any virtue, and if there be any praise, think on these things"* (Philippians 4:8 KJV).

Negative words come from a negative attitude and pollute the atmosphere of faith. Instead of allowing the stock market or plummeting economy to be your focus of conversation, I encourage you to look to Jesus, the Author and Finisher of your faith. Hebrews 10:35 admonishes, *"Cast not away your confidence, which has great recompense of reward."*

RECOGNIZE SATAN'S STRATEGY

Know your enemy. Don't be afraid of him, just know his tactics. Be aware of his strategy. *"The thief cometh not but to steal and kill and destroy"* (John 10:10). If Satan can find any crack in the door of your life, he will force open the door. Strong Christians who are godly on every other front are often the most vulnerable in the area of money.

Fearing poverty is one kind of bondage. But financial prosperity can also be a snare to our souls. Money is as dangerous as dynamite with the fuse lit— an explosive powder with the power to destroy. All through the Scriptures you can see how a wrong focus on money wreaked havoc, both in the church and in personal lives. Achan, Gehazi, Elisha's servant, Judas, Ananias and Sapphira—all of them were destroyed because of money. Watch out that you don't grab at the shadow and miss out on the substance of the very life God has for you.

GUARD YOUR PRAYER LIFE

In Spanish, we have two verbs for the word *know*. One is to know about a thing or person; the other has to do with an intimate knowledge or relationship. Most people know more *about* God than they have *experienced* God. Prayer requires time and discipline, but it is the only way you will become acquainted with your Father.

Martha and I have been sustained by prayer for more than half a century of mission work. It has been the key to God's guidance, provision, and divine miracles in the area of giving and receiving. The Bible exhorts us to pray without ceasing, to pray in the Holy Ghost, to pray on all occasions. There is nothing more crucial to your walk of faith than developing and sustaining a fervent prayer life. You can do more than pray *after* you have prayed, but you can never do more than pray *until* you have prayed.

LIVE WITH A SENSE OF DESTINY

Someone once said that unless you see the ultimate, you will be enslaved by the immediate. God wants our life, not on a time-payment plan, but all at once. Living as a person with purpose will cause you to be consumed with God's perspective of the world. It's the kind of passion that caused Esther to say, "If I perish, I perish."

We are like her—called to the kingdom for this hour—and God intends that we fulfill our destiny. When we make a commitment to go the distance, He promises to provide everything we need.

Supply has never been a problem to God. What God ordains, He sustains; where He leads, He feeds. God is no man's debtor. If we walk in obedience to Him, He always has a few "handfuls of purpose" (Ruth 2:16) in addition to His normal supply.

RUN TO WIN

"The just live by faith" (Galatians 3:11). Living a life of faith all the way to the end is a lifestyle that will make you a winner. God is able to do what He has already begun in your life. He wants to see you finish triumphantly.

You are a son or a daughter of God. You have a lawyer, an advocate in Jesus Christ, who has never lost a case. He represents you, interceding to the Father for you. The precious Holy Spirit resides in you—that same Spirit that raised Jesus from the dead.

I think of all those anointed ones who have left big footprints in the nations of the world: David Livingstone, William Carey, Adoniram Judson, Jonathan Goforth, C.T. Studd—they all accomplished the plan of God for their lives and left a legacy behind them in the process. They did it by giving their energy, their finances, and their lives. God has always had a people who have not bowed down to this world's idols—the lust of the eye or the pride of life.

As for me, I plan to be in the winner's circle. I haven't arrived, but I feel like I'm on third base. I can see home plate. I know I'm going to score by the grace of God, and I'm going to score standing up. I refuse to slide in under the catcher—it has cost too much to come this far to be put out of the game between third and home plate. Besides, when you get put out between third and home plate, you add nothing to the score.

I will leave this world the same way I came in—with nothing. Until then, my life's goal is to keep on practicing a lifestyle of *living to give*. It is the only way to keep storing up my treasures in heaven, where there is no recession, depreciation, rust, or decay.

The goal of our faith is to hear God say, "Well done, my child. I gave you a job to do and you did it—come on in."

To contact Wayne Myers:
The Great Commission Evangelistic Association
P. O. Box 764247
Dallas, TX   75376-4247

To Order Wayne Myer's
Books contact:
lbtpossible@live.com